Selected Studies from

PROVERBS

Insight for Living
Bible Study Guide

From the Bible-teaching ministry of

Charles R. Swindoll

INSIGHT FOR LIVING

Chuck graduated in 1963 from Dallas Theological Seminary, where he now serves as the school's fourth president, helping to prepare a new generation of men and women for the ministry. Chuck has served in pastorates in three states: Massachusetts, Texas, and California, including almost twenty-three years at the First Evangelical Free Church in Fullerton, California. He is currently senior pastor of Stonebriar Community Church in Frisco, Texas, north of Dallas. His sermon messages have been aired over radio since 1979 as the *Insight for Living* broadcast. A best-selling author, Chuck has written numerous books and booklets on many subjects.

Based on the outlines and transcripts of Chuck's sermons, the study guide text is co-authored by Lee Hough, a graduate of the University of Texas at Arlington and Dallas Theological Seminary. He also wrote the Living Insights sections.

Editor in Chief: Cynthia Swindoll	**Text Designer:** Gary Lett
Coauthor of Text: Lee Hough	**Graphic System Administrator:** Bob Haskins
Senior Editor: Wendy Peterson	**Director, Communications Division:** John Norton
Copy Editors: Deborah Gibbs Cheryl Gilmore Karla Lenderink Glenda Schlahta Marco Salazar	**Production Manager:** Don Bernstein **Printer:** Sinclair Printing Company

Unless otherwise identified, all Scripture references are from the New American Standard Bible, updated edition, copyright © The Lockman Foundation 1960, 1962, 1963, 1968, 1971, 1972, 1973, 1975, 1977. Used by permission. Scripture taken from the Holy Bible, New International Version, Copyright © 1973, 1978, 1984 International Bible Society, used by permission of Zondervan Bible Publishers [NIV]. Scripture taken from *The New Testament: A Private Translation in the Language of the People* by Charles B. Williams (Chicago, Ill.: Moody Press, 1958), [WILLIAMS]. The other translations cited are the *Living Bible* [LB], and *The Message*.

CONTENTS

INTRODUCTION

We often refer to the faith of Abraham, the patience of Job, and the courage of Elijah. As we turn to the ancient book of Proverbs, we come to the wisdom of Solomon.

I have never (and I mean *never*) opened my Bible to Proverbs without finding a principle or insight that gave me just what I needed at the moment. This book is not only wise, it is rele-vant and timely . . . constantly up to date. And my, how convicting!

As we undertake this very practical study of selected proverbs, my desire is that you will realize anew how aware God is of your circumstances. May you and I both gain a whole new perspective on life as a result of these days we spend together, drinking in the pure, clean, and wholesome water of the Word. May we be nour-ished in our walk with the Lord!

The wisdom of Solomon need not remain within the lines of Proverbs. May it soon be seen in your life and mine.

Chuck Swindoll

PUTTING TRUTH INTO ACTION

K nowledge apart from application falls short of God's desire for His children. He wants us to apply what we learn so that we will change and grow. This study guide was prepared with these goals in mind. As you go through the following pages, we hope your desire to discover biblical truth will grow as your understanding of God's Word increases and that you will be encouraged to apply what you've learned.

To assist you in your study, we've included a section called Living Insights at the end of each lesson. These exercises will challenge you to study further and to think of specific ways to put your discoveries into action.

There are many ways to use this guide—in personal devotions, group studies, discussions with friends and family, and Sunday school classes. And, of course, it's an ideal study aid when you're listening to its corresponding *Insight for Living* radio series.

To benefit most from this study guide, we would encourage you to consider it a spiritual journal. That's why we've included space in the Living Insights for recording your thoughts and discoveries. We hope you'll return to those sections often for review and encouragement as you continue to grow in your walk with Christ.

Insight for Living

Selected Studies from

PROVERBS

Chapter 1

VERTICAL WISDOM FOR HORIZONTAL LIVING

Proverbs 1:1–9

Since 1955 knowledge has doubled every five years; libraries groan with the weight of new books. . . . In fact, our generation possesses more data about the universe and human personality than all previous generations put together. High school graduates today have been exposed to more information about the world than Plato, Aristotle, Spinoza or Benjamin Franklin. In terms of facts alone, neither Moses nor Paul could pass a college entrance exam today.

Yet by everyone's standards, even with all our knowledge . . . society today is peopled with a bumper crop of brilliant failures. . . . Men and women educated to earn a living often don't know anything about handling life itself. Alumni from noted universities have mastered information about a narrow slice of life but couldn't make it out of the first grade when it comes to living successfully with family and friends. Let's face it. Knowledge is not enough to meet life's problems. We need wisdom, the ability to handle life with skill.[1]

Where can we find this rare, intangible quality—and how? By drawing from the wealth of practical insights divinely deposited in the book of Proverbs. Unlike the Psalms, which deepen

---

1. Haddon Robinson, from the foreword to Robert L. Alden's *Proverbs: A Commentary on an Ancient Book of Timeless Advice* (Grand Rapids, Mich.: Baker Book House, 1983), p. 7.

our devotional life with God, Proverbs enriches our ability to cope with daily life and other people.

Do you need wisdom so you can become skilled at godly living? Then become a student of Proverbs, one of the richest volumes of vertical wisdom for horizontal living ever written.

To begin, let's conduct a general survey of the book's origin and purposes. Then, in subsequent chapters, we'll focus our energies on finding valuable principles of wisdom related to practical living.

The Name of the Book

Clearly visible on the surface of verse 1 are the name and author of the book: "The proverbs of Solomon the son of David, king of Israel." Commentator Robert Alden writes, "Just as we associate the law with Moses and David with the Psalms, so we put wisdom and Solomon together."[2] Solomon, however, did not compose the entire book. Chapter 30, for example, was penned by an individual named Agur (v. 1), and the insights of chapter 31 were taught to King Lemuel by his mother (v. 1).

The name Proverbs comes from the Hebrew root word *mashal*, meaning "to represent, be like." It connotes making a comparison to convey a specific truth in a pointed way. The book is filled with sayings, many brief, to guide the life of the godly. One person defined these pithy sayings as "short sentences drawn from long experience."

The Contents of the Book

The capsules of truth presented in Proverbs come mostly in one of three kinds of couplets. Some are *contrastive*, using the word *but*, as in 13:1:

[handwritten: parallel both sides of the angle]

A wise son accepts his father's discipline,
But a scoffer does not listen to rebuke.
(see also vv. 10, 18, 24)

Others are *completive*, using the words *and* or *so*, as in 14:10:

The heart knows its own bitterness,
And a stranger does not share its joy.
(see also v. 13; 16:3)

2. Alden, *Proverbs*, p. 19.

Handwritten top: Pear-filled w/ all different types of men — women children

Handwritten: *NOT A BOOK OF THEORY.

And still others are *comparative*, using the words *better/than* or *like/so*, as in 15:16–17: *(handwritten: pickrisk)*

> Better is a little with the fear of the Lord,
> Than great treasure and turmoil with it.
> Better is a dish of vegetables where love is,
> Than a fattened ox and hatred with it.
> (see also 25:24–25)

In addition to using couplets to impart truth, Solomon also relies on the cameo appearances of a wide cast of characters.[3] Together, the couplets and characters help prepare us to deal wisely with life's knotty issues. As psychologist Jay Adams points out, there are basically four ways of dealing with problems: (1) we can avoid them; (2) we can allow them to deflect us from our goals; (3) we can view our situation as hopeless and simply give up; or (4) we can work through the issue to a healthy resolution.[4]

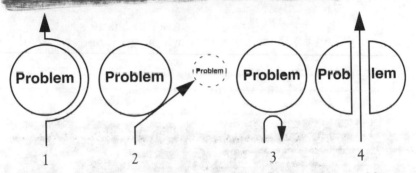

Proverbs is filled with direct, practical counsel that enables its readers to choose option four illustrated above. For example, to deal with the problem of lust, Solomon advises:

> Reproofs for discipline are the way of life,
> To keep you from the evil woman,
> From the smooth tongue of the adulteress.
> Do not desire her beauty in your heart,
> Nor let her catch you with her eyelids. (6:23b–25)

---

3. From a personal study on counseling in Proverbs, Chuck once counted forty-six specific kinds of men, twenty-three kinds of women, and several types of children.

4. See Jay E. Adams, *Competent to Counsel* (Phillipsburg, N.J.: Presbyterian and Reformed Publishing Co., 1970), pp. 129–30.

The context is that of a father speaking to his son, and his words cut right through to a solution: To resist lust's temptations, you must guard your heart. In other words, do not meditate on impure thoughts. Do not cultivate base imaginations. Don't linger with lustful eyes. Solomon doesn't engage in wishful thinking or abstract theorizing; he gives inspired, straightforward help.

The Purposes of the Book

Now let's dig a little deeper into chapter 1 and uncover the five specific purposes of Proverbs.

> To know wisdom and instruction,
> To discern the sayings of understanding,
> To receive instruction in wise behavior,
> Righteousness, justice and equity;
> To give prudence to the naive,
> To the youth knowledge and discretion,
> A wise man will hear and increase in learning,
> And a man of understanding will acquire wise
>   counsel,
> To understand a proverb and a figure,
> The words of the wise and their riddles.
> (vv. 2–6)

First: *To revere and obey God from the heart.* Solomon reveals his first purpose in verse 2a, "to know wisdom and instruction." The term *wisdom* is key to this book, so let's examine its meaning with the help of commentator Sid Buzzell.

Of the several words for wisdom and related synonyms used in Proverbs, the primary and most frequent one is *hokmâh*. It occurs 45 times in Proverbs. In the Old Testament *hokmâh* is used of the skill of craftsmen, sailors, singers, mourners, administrators, and counselors. These workers and others, being knowledgeable, experienced, and efficient in their areas of expertise, were considered skillful; they were therefore "wise." Similarly in the spiritual realm a person who possesses *hokmâh* in reference to God is one who is both knowledgeable and experienced in following God's way. So in the Bible's Wisdom literature being wise means being skilled in godly living. Having God's wisdom means having the ability to cope with life in a God-honoring way.[5]

Closely connected to wisdom is our need for "instruction." More than just the communication of facts, the term Solomon uses for this word means "discipline, chastening, or correction." The person who is wise in godly living exercises moral discipline. As commentator Derek Kidner points out, "Wisdom will be hard-won, a quality of character as much as of mind."[6]

Second: To provide discernment to the eye. This next purpose comes from the second half of verse 2, "To discern the sayings of understanding." *Discern* means "understand, consider, perceive."[7] It's the ability to read between the lines, to distinguish truth from error, right from wrong, good from evil (see 1 Kings 3:9). The *Theological Wordbook of the Old Testament* adds that it is "a power of judgment and perceptive insight and is demonstrated in the use of knowledge."[8] A little later in this same source we're also told that,

> insight or moral understanding is a gift from God (Dan 2:21) and is not the fruit of empiricism. It is ethical discernment. A person prays for it (Ps 119:34) and since this insight is uniquely God's, he can reveal or conceal it (Isa 29:14). . . .
>
> While understanding it is a gift of God, it does not come automatically. The possession of it requires a persistent diligence. It is more than IQ; it connotes character. One is at fault if he doesn't have it and in fact, not to pursue it will incur God's punishment (Prov 2:1f; Ruth 1:21f).[9]

5. Sid S. Buzzell, "Proverbs," in *The Bible Knowledge Commentary*, Old Testament ed., ed. John F. Walvoord and Roy B. Zuck (Colorado Springs, Colo.: Chariot Victor Publishing, 1985), p. 902.

6. Derek Kidner, *The Proverbs: An Introduction and Commentary* (Downers Grove, Ill.: Inter-Varsity Press, 1964), p. 36.

7. R. Laird Harris, Gleason L. Archer, Jr., and Bruce K. Waltke, eds., *Theological Wordbook of the Old Testament* (Chicago, Ill.: Moody Press, 1980), vol. 1, p. 103.

8. Harris, Archer, and Waltke, *Theological Wordbook*, vol. 1, p. 103.

9. Harris, Archer, and Waltke, *Theological Wordbook*, vol. 1, pp. 103–4.

Third: To develop alertness in the walk. We are, according to Proverbs 1:3,

> To receive instruction in wise behavior,
> Righteousness, justice, and equity.

The word *receive* "suggests action or mobility. It's the term associated with 'plucking grapes and taking them with you.' In this instance, it refers to instruction that is to be plucked and taken like succulent fruit from a vine."[10]

Fourth: To establish discretion and purpose in life. This objective is somewhat different from the others because we're told in verse 4 the kind of persons Proverbs will benefit most.

> To give prudence to the naive.
> To the youth knowledge and discretion.

In its root form, the Hebrew term for *naive* means to "be open, spacious, wide."[11] The simple person is wide open, easily influenced, gullible; an easy target for someone such as the harlot described in chapter 7. As for the "youth" Solomon mentions, this refers to anyone between birth and marriageable age—small children, early adolescent teens, young adults. PROV 22:6

What will Proverbs do for the simple and the young? (1) The naive will become prudent, which *Webster's* defines as being "shrewd in the management of practical affairs."[12] Prudent individuals demonstrate good common sense. And (2) for the young who practice the wisdom of Proverbs, the reward is "discretion." C. H. Toy defines this as "the power of forming plans."[13] Derek Kidner adds,

> The godly man is in the best sense a man of affairs,
> who takes the trouble to know his way about, and
> plan his course realistically (*cf.* 22:3: "a shrewd man
> sees danger and hides himself; but the simple go on,
> and suffer for it").[14]

10. From the study guide *You and Your Problems*, coauthored by Lee Hough, from the Bible-teaching ministry of Charles R. Swindoll (Fullerton, Calif.: Insight for Living, 1989), p. 3.

11. R. Laird Harris, Gleason L. Archer, Jr., and Bruce K. Waltke, eds., *Theological Wordbook of the Old Testament* (Chicago, Ill.: Moody Press, 1980), vol. 2, p. 742.

12. *Merriam-Webster's Collegiate Dictionary*, 10th ed., see "prudent."

13. C. H. Toy, as quoted by Kidner in *Proverbs*, p. 37.

14. Kidner, *Proverbs*, p. 37.

> To understand a proverb and a figure,
> The words of the wise and their riddles.

According to Buzzell, "the word for 'riddle' (*hîdâh*) means an indirect, oblique, or enigmatic statement (like a figure of speech) which needs interpretation."[15] An in-depth study of Proverbs will "introduce the reader to a style of teaching that provokes his thought, getting under his skin by thrusts of wit, paradox, common sense and teasing symbolism."[16] Exercising our minds in such a variety of ways will inevitably sharpen our ability to think deeply and with versatility.

The Goal of the Book

In closing, notice three key sources of wisdom mentioned in Proverbs 1:7–9.

> The fear of the Lord is the beginning of knowledge;
> Fools despise wisdom and instruction.
> Hear, my son, your father's instruction,
> And do not forsake your mother's teaching;
> Indeed, they are a graceful wreath to your head,
> And ornaments about your neck.

The fear of the Lord, a father's instruction, and a mother's teaching—all three impart wisdom. And wisdom is not a burdensome load that will weigh down your life but a treasure that will add grace and beauty to your days.

 Living Insights STUDY ONE

To begin gathering the wealth of wisdom in Proverbs, focus your attention right now and memorize Proverbs 1:7.

> The fear of the Lord is the beginning of knowledge;
> Fools despise wisdom and instruction.

15. Buzzell, "Proverbs," p. 907.

16. Kidner, *Proverbs*, pp. 58–59.

Next, listen to LeRoy Eims as he explains the rich meaning behind the concept of fearing God.

What does this expression mean? Some say it means reverential trust, or affectionate reverence. . . .

Let us not forget, however, that when God gave His law to His people, He did so to the accompaniment of thunder and lightning and thick smoke. The people at the foot of Mount Sinai trembled. When we think of the fear of the Lord, let us not eliminate altogether the plain old "being afraid of God." Remember the words of the New Testament, "It is a fearful thing to fall into the hands of the living God" (Heb. 10:31).

The first result of this godly fear is that God must be reverenced for who He is. . . .

Second, God is to be served. If He is truly Almighty God, if we are His people, if we are living in His Word through a daily experience with Him, it behooves each one of us to find our place of service to Him and joyfully give our lives to the responsibility God has placed before us.

Third, God is to be worshiped. Jesus, in His encounter with the woman at the well of Sychar in Samaria, told her, "But the hour cometh, and now is, when the true worshipers shall worship the Father in spirit and in truth, for the Father seeketh such to worship Him. God is a Spirit, and they that worship Him must worship Him in spirit and in truth" (John 4:23–24).

Fourth, God is to be obeyed. Solomon also wrote, "Let us hear the conclusion of the whole matter: fear God, and keep His commandments, for this is the whole duty of man. For God shall bring every work into judgment, with every secret thing, whether it be good, or whether it be evil" (Eccles. 12:13–14).

Because of all that God has done for us in His grace and mercy, showered on us in Jesus Christ, we are to love Him with all our hearts, souls, and minds. The Apostle John taught, "We love Him because He first loved us" (1 John 4:19). So when you add it all up, that we should reverence God, serve Him, worship Him, obey Him, and love Him, that is a picture of the beginning of knowledge. And only fools despise it.[17]

Do you "fear the Lord"? In this next Living Insight, let's search for this precious attitude in the daily flow of our own lives.

Living Insights

STUDY TWO

Pause for a moment to think about this past week and identify the practical ways in which you reverenced the Lord. If you need help knowing what to look for, reread the five results of fearing God that LeRoy Eims noted in the first Living Insight.

_____

_____

_____

_____

_____

_____

_____

_____

What are some of the ways you've seen other believers demonstrate a fear of the Lord?

_____

_____

_____

17. LeRoy Eims, _Wisdom from Above_ (Wheaton, Ill.: Scripture Press Publications, Victor Books, 1978), pp. 17–18.

9

_____

_____

_____

_____

_____

_____

Is there something you want to imitate or adapt to strengthen your fear of the Lord?

_____

_____

_____

_____

_____

_____

_____

_____

———————◆———————

To enrich your exploration of Proverbs, read one chapter a day for the next thirty-one days—starting today!

Chapter 2

WARNINGS AGAINST REFUSING REPROOF

Proverbs 1:20–33

We began our study of Proverbs in the last chapter "by breaking up the plain daylight of wisdom (*hokmá*) into its rainbow of constituent colours."[1] Instruction, discernment, prudence—these are but a few of the many shades of wisdom we examined.

Now let's familiarize ourselves with wisdom from a completely different perspective. Beginning in verse 20 of chapter 1, Solomon presents wisdom to us as a person. No longer just an abstract principle to be dissected with definitions, wisdom now speaks to us personified as a woman.

Some Basic Facts about Wisdom

Allow us to acquaint you with certain facts about "Lady Wisdom."

First: Wisdom Is Available

Wisdom shouts in the street,
She lifts her voice in the square;
At the head of the noisy streets she cries out;
At the entrance of the gates in the city, she
    utters her sayings. (vv. 20–21)

Wisdom is not shy. As you can see, she's very accessible and easy to find. In fact, she goes out of her way to speak to us through God's Word, creation, and the lessons of daily life.

Second: Wisdom Can Be Ignored and Spurned

"I called, and you refused;
I stretched out my hand, and no one paid attention;
And you neglected all my counsel,
And did not want my reproof." (vv. 24–25)

Our problem is not exposure to wisdom—our problem is putting

---

1. Derek Kidner, *The Proverbs: An Introduction and Commentary* (Downers Grove, Ill.: Inter-Varsity Press, 1964), p. 36.

her words into practice. So often we stroll by wisdom's outstretched hand, tossing a careless "No, thank you" over our shoulders as we crane our necks to find someone with more pleasing ideas (see 2 Tim. 4:2–4). Proverbs 1:22 names three types of individuals who consistently shun wisdom.

> "How long, O naive ones, will you love simplicity?
> And scoffers delight themselves in scoffing,
> And fools hate knowledge?"

The naive. As you may recall from the first lesson, the naive or simple individual lacks discernment. He or she is easily enchanted by the music of pied pipers, blindly following them wherever they lead.

The scoffer. This is the skeptic, the mocker, someone who contemptuously disagrees with anything that opposes his or her own ideas.

The fool. Typically, when we think of a fool, we picture someone who lacks intelligence. But the biblical meaning of fool is "not so much one lacking in mental powers, as one who misuses them; not one who does not reason, but reasons wrongly."[2]

Third: Wisdom Spurned Bears Serious Consequences

> "Because I called and you refused; . . .
> I will even laugh at your calamity;
> I will mock when your dread comes,
> When your dread comes like a storm,
> And your calamity comes on like a whirlwind,
> When distress and anguish come on you.
> Then they will call on me, but I will not answer;
> They will seek me diligently, but they shall not
>   find me, . . .
> So they shall eat of the fruit of their own way,
> And be satiated with their own devices.
> For the waywardness of the naive shall kill them,
> And the complacency of fools shall destroy
>   them." (vv. 24a, 26–28, 31–32)

When we've rejected wisdom's healthy counsel month after month, year after year, and sated ourselves instead on the world's artificially sweetened advice, we can expect some heartburn. But God doesn't offer any panic packages of wisdom that can plop-plop-fizz-fizz our

---

2. Merrill F. Unger, *Unger's Bible Dictionary*, 3d ed. (Chicago, Ill.: Moody Press, 1966), p. 375.

problems away. It'll take a careful new diet and strenuous exercise to shape up those sour situations and distorted values.[3] How much better to heed wisdom's counsel from the beginning and reap the rewards promised in verse 33:

> "But he who listens to me shall live securely,
> And shall be at ease from the dread of evil."

The Connection between Wisdom and Reproof

Let's shift our attention away from Lady Wisdom herself now and focus instead on how she comes to us. What avenue does God frequently use to get our attention so that we'll heed her voice? See if you can pick out the answer that's repeated in these three verses.

> "Turn to my reproof,
> Behold, I will pour out my spirit on you;
> I will make my words known to you. . . .
> And you neglected all my counsel,
> And did not want my reproof; . . .
> They would not accept my counsel,
> They spurned all my reproof." (vv. 23, 25, 30)

If you guessed "reproof," you're right. Wisdom comes to us when we accept and adjust to God's reproofs, that is to say, His reprimands, cautions, and counsel. Commentator Robert Alden notes,

> Criticism is hard to take; few respond to it with ease. It is ego-damaging, yet accepting it and changing in response to it is the only way to succeed. Soil must be plowed, harrowed, and broken before it can be used. Clay must be kneaded and pounded before it can be shaped into a useful or beautiful vessel. People too must sometimes be broken in order to have bad habits and attitudes replaced with good ones. Blessed are those who take this sage's advice and listen to criticism.[4]

---

3. Adapted from the study guide *You and Your Problems*, coauthored by Lee Hough, from the Bible-teaching ministry of Charles R. Swindoll (Fullerton, Calif.: Insight for Living, 1989), pp. 4–5.

4. Robert L. Alden, *Proverbs: A Commentary on an Ancient Book of Timeless Advice* (Grand Rapids, Mich.: Baker Book House, 1983), p. 28.

Sometimes God's reproofs come to us *directly* through His Word:

"For the commandment is a lamp, and the teaching is a light;
And reproofs for discipline are the way of life."
(Prov. 6:23; see also Ps. 119:33–40 and
2 Tim. 3:16–17)

The Lord also uses *indirect* means to correct us, such as life's experiences or other people. For example, when your child says, "Dad, aren't you supposed to stop on red?" Or when everyone else arrives at the meeting on time except you. Or when you drive by a jogger after you've overeaten at a restaurant.

What qualities are these direct and indirect reproofs designed to develop in us? Here are just a few for you to ponder.

Alertness	Discernment	Love	Sincerity
Appreciation	Discipline	Loyalty	Submissiveness
Compassion	Efficiency	Objectivity	Tactfulness
Confidentiality	Enthusiasm	Patience	Teachability
Consistency	Flexibility	Peacefulness	Thoroughness
Cooperativeness	Gentleness	Punctuality	Thoughtfulness
Courtesy	Honesty	Self-control	Tolerance
Creativity	Humility	Sense of Humor	Understanding
Dependability	Initiative	Sensitivity	Unselfishness

Don't let this list overwhelm you; instead, let it be an inspiration!

Why Reproof Is Refused

Unfortunately, Christians who humbly accept reproof are rare. Why? At least four reasons can be gleaned on a closer inspection of verses 24–25 in Proverbs 1.

1. *Willful refusal:* "Because I called, and you refused" (v. 24a). Wisdom is speaking—she entreats you and me to receive her counsel, but often we deliberately ignore her. Not because we fail to hear her or misunderstand her words; rather, it's because we're sinful and self-centered and hate to bow the knee to anyone's authority except our own.

For an even clearer picture of just how stubborn this kind of rejection is, consider this: the same word for *refused* used here is also used of Pharaoh when he refused to let Israel go despite God's repeated reproofs (see Exod. 4:23; 7:14; 10:3).

2. *Insensitivity:* "I stretched out my hand, and no one paid

14

attention" (Prov. 1:24b). To be insensitive means to lack aware-ness or alertness. It corresponds with the New Testament phrase, "dull of hearing" (Heb. 5:11; compare Matt. 13:15). Reproofs come, but we're not even aware of them. We're not sensitive to God's correction through His Word or other people. Why? Oftentimes it's because we're so preoccupied with life. Financial pressures, work woes, and relational rifts overwhelm us, and we become like horses wearing blinders, seeing only the problems straight in front of us. Then, too, there's sometimes the problem of overexposure to church. After years of sitting in the same pew, the truths of Scripture are so familiar to some of us that our hearts have stopped really hearing them.

3. *Indifference:* "And you neglected all my counsel" (Prov. 1:25a). The indifferent person says, "Point out all the wrong about me you like, I just don't care." People who respond in this manner are often depressed. Look, for example, at 15:32, where the same term for *neglects* is used and notice how the indifferent individual is described:

> He who neglects discipline despises himself,
> But he who listens to reproof acquires understanding.

Depression can induce people to despise themselves so deeply that they carelessly shrug their shoulders at reproof because nothing really seems to matter anymore—or else things seem so bad that they've decided to just give up.

4. *Defensiveness:* "And did not want my reproof" (1:25b). Instead of admitting wrong, some people vigorously defend their deficien-cies. You've heard the excuses before—"But you don't understand!" or, "I don't deserve this!" or, "I can't help it, it's just the way I am." No matter how clearly wrong these individuals are, they simply won't admit fault. In their minds it's always the other person who should change.

Willful refusal, insensitivity, indifference, defensiveness—are any of these an uncomfortable reminder of the way you reacted to a recent reproof? Perhaps the correction came from a parent, a pastor, a teacher, or even a letter from a friend. We all know how painful those times can be. But just remember, only those sensitive and responsive to Lady Wisdom enjoy the reward of skillful godly living.

May these words from the writer of Hebrews encourage you to embrace wisdom the next time she calls.

> All discipline for the moment seems not to be joyful,
> but sorrowful; yet to those who have been trained

by it, afterwards it yields the peaceful fruit of righteousness. (Heb. 12:11)

 Living Insights _____

> It's a wise man who profits by his own experience,
> but it's a good deal wiser one who lets the rattlesnake
> bite the other fellow.[5]

Let's examine the snakebites of others who ignored wisdom's
reproofs and walked right into a viper's den of painful consequences.
We've already mentioned Pharaoh as an example of willful refusal.
Can you think of another, not only for this category but also for the
other three? In case you need help, here are a few passages to get
you started: Genesis 4:1–9; 1 Samuel 3:11–18; 15:1–28; Matthew
19:16–24; 23:13–37.

Willful refusal:

_____

_____

_____

Insensitivity:

_____

_____

_____

Indifference:

_____

_____

_____

5. Henry Wheeler Shaw, as quoted in *The International Dictionary of Thoughts,* comp. John P.
Bradley, Leo F. Daniels, and Thomas C. Jones (Chicago, Ill.: J. G. Ferguson Publishing Co.,
1969), p. 774.

Defensiveness:

_____

_____

_____

Living Insights

No matter how we refuse reproof, whether willfully, indifferently, or in some other way, the reason for it is usually the same—self-protection. None of us likes admitting to faults, because our sense of self-worth is directly tied to our performance. Wisdom's reproofs threaten our ego.

But what if . . . what if we changed our basic goal in life? What if, instead of protecting ourselves, we committed ourselves to becoming like Christ? How would we respond to wisdom then? Defensively? Indifferently? Not hardly. When conformity to Christ becomes our deep-seated desire, we welcome reproof. Sure, it's still painful at times, but that's because our old self hates being passed over in favor of the new self being created in the image of Christ (see Col. 3:9–10).

Tell me what you know about self-protection. How does it manifest itself in your responses to reproof?

_____

_____

_____

_____

_____

Based on the way you typically respond to reproof, what would you say is your goal? Self-protection or Christlikeness?

Chapter 3

FOR MINERS ONLY

Proverbs 2:1–9

A s we delve more deeply into the rich wisdom of Proverbs, we come to a sign posted above the entrance of Proverbs 2 that reads: FOR MINERS ONLY. It's the end of the line for the tourist and the timid. Only those willing to wear the hard hat of commitment are encouraged to go beyond this point. From now on the digging becomes more personal and intense.

Are you still eager to move forward? Then let's enter chapter 2, where we'll be given four tools and the training to use them to extract King Solomon's treasures.

The Conditions

The first tool handed to us is in the couplet of verse 1.

Discipline of the Written Word

My son, . . . receive my sayings,
And treasure my commandments within you.

The "sayings" and "commandments" are God's Word, and to wield it correctly in our mining efforts we must do two things.

First, *possess the right attitude toward God's Word.* Our attitude toward the Bible determines virtually everything about how skillfully we live the Christian life. If we're receptive, eager to take the Scriptures into our hands, our reward will be great. But if we flippantly ignore it, we'll be no more successful at finding His riches than if we tried to pry precious gems from rocks with our bare hands.

Second, *saturate your mind with God's Word.* Long ago the prophet Hosea lamented, "My people are destroyed for lack of knowledge" (4:6). The Israelites neglected to store up the Law in their hearts, and they starved spiritually. The right handling of God's Word includes hearing, reading, studying, memorizing, and meditating on it. Such diligent cultivation will result in a rich harvest of wisdom—and that is one treasure the Lord wants us to hoard (see also Ps. 119:11).

Discipline of Inner Desire

Moving on to the next couplet, we find our second tool.

18

Make your ear attentive to wisdom,
Incline your heart to understanding. (Prov. 2:2)

Lose this tool, this longing for God's wisdom, and we face the peril A. W. Tozer wrote of in his book *The Divine Conquest*.

> Is it not true that for most of us who call ourselves Christians there is no real experience? We have substituted theological ideas for an arresting encounter; we are full of religious notions, but our great weakness is that for our hearts there is no one there.
>
> Whatever else it embraces, true Christian experience must always include a genuine encounter with God. Without this, religion is but a shadow, a reflection of reality, a cheap copy of an original once enjoyed by someone else of whom we have heard.[1]

What must we do to dig for wisdom with the right motivation, rather than only go through the motions of mining and end up empty-handed?

First, *have an attentive ear*. Have you ever been near a mom in a bustling home when she suddenly says, "Excuse me, my baby's crying, I need to go check on her," but all you hear is the babel of people talking? Isn't it amazing how sensitively tuned a parent's ear can be to a child's voice? We can develop that same keen receptivity toward our heavenly Father by honing a sensitive ear to His reproofs. Ask God to make you attentive to wisdom's voice.

Second, *cultivate an open heart*. With the ear we receive wisdom and with the heart we store it up. But not just any heart can hold this particular kind of treasure. Only one that is *inclined*—stretched out, opened up—has such a capacity.

Discipline of Prevailing Prayer

The third tool to become familiar with is found in the couplet of verse 3.

. . . Cry for discernment,
Lift your voice for understanding.

Perhaps the most difficult mining tool to master is consistent, fervent prayer. It's said that Martin Luther set apart the three best

---

1. A. W. Tozer, *The Divine Conquest* (Camp Hill, Pa.: Christian Publications, 1978), p. 26.

19

hours of his day to pray. Most of us, however, can't imagine spending thirty minutes even on our best day. What can we do to improve?

First, *proclaim the need for discernment*. How many of us have wasted our time wishing for discernment instead of actually asking God for it through prayer? "You do not have because you do not ask," James pointedly reminds us (James 4:2b). And the same is also true concerning Solomon's second exhortation.

Second, *request understanding*. James has also said that "if any of you lacks wisdom, let him ask of God, who gives to all men generously and without reproach, and it will be given to him" (1:5). Who do we ask? Where do we look for wisdom? God! He is the source we must earnestly beseech for the wisdom we need (read Job 28:1, 12–15, 20–21, 23–24, 28). Can we honestly say that we do?

Discipline of Daily Consistency

Finally, the couplet in Proverbs 2:4 brings us our last tool.

> . . . Seek her as silver,
> And search for her as for hidden treasures.

All of us have our hot and cold moments spiritually, but to become successful miners of God's wisdom we must have some measure of consistency about our daily digging. For that to happen, remember these two tips.

First, *seek wisdom with diligence*, and second, *pursue it with patience*. The Hebrew term for *seek* doesn't connote a glance here or there. It's the idea of a person relentlessly searching for something with the full expectation of finding it.[2] Mining is demanding work. The precious stones of discernment and understanding are "not usually discovered by a casual observer or chance passerby. They are excavated and enjoyed instead by the diligent, devoted, and determined."[3]

The Results

What happens *if* we receive Solomon's sayings (v. 1), and *if* we cry to God for discernment (v. 3), and *if* we seek understanding as

2. R. Laird Harris, Gleason L. Archer, Jr., and Bruce K. Waltke, eds., *Theological Wordbook of the Old Testament* (Chicago, Ill.: Moody Press, 1980), vol. 1, p. 129.

3. Robert L. Alden, *Proverbs: A Commentary on an Ancient Book of Timeless Advice* (Grand Rapids, Mich.: Baker Book House, 1983), p. 32.

silver (v. 4)? Verse 5 announces our reward:

> Then you will discern the fear of the Lord,
> And discover the knowledge of God.

The prize we seek is twofold. "The fear of the Lord"—a deep, awesome respect, and "the knowledge of God"—a bosom nearness to Him. Derek Kidner wonderfully describes these as "the poles of awe and intimacy."[4] Read carefully Tozer's explanation of how saints throughout time have experienced these two rewards.

> The spiritual giants of old were [those] who at some time became acutely conscious of the real Presence of God and maintained that consciousness for the rest of their lives. The first encounter may have been one of terror, as when a "horror of great darkness" fell upon Abram, or as when Moses at the bush hid his face because he was afraid to look upon God. Usually this fear soon lost its content of terror and changed after a while to delightsome awe, to level off finally into a reverent sense of complete nearness to God.[5]

The Promises

Mining has always been a risky endeavor. The lure of fabulous riches has left many a prospector penniless. So what surety do we have that, if we dig as Solomon has directed, we will discover the rich rewards promised in verse 5? Our guarantee is explained in verses 6–9:

> For the Lord gives wisdom;
> From His mouth come knowledge and
>   understanding.
> He stores up sound wisdom for the upright;
> He is a shield to those who walk in integrity,
> Guarding the paths of justice,
> And He preserves the way of His godly ones.

4. Derek Kidner, The Proverbs: An Introduction and Commentary (Downers Grove, Ill.: Inter-Varsity Press, 1964), p. 61.

5. Tozer, The Divine Conquest, pp. 26–27.

> Then you will discern righteousness and justice
> And equity and every good course.

If we faithfully apply the mining tools and procedures outlined thus far, we can count on at least three benefits. First, *from within:* our hearts will be filled with wisdom, knowledge, and understanding (vv. 6–7a). Second, *from without:* God will provide protection (vv. 7b–8). This implies that we shall certainly encounter opposition, but the Lord promises to shield us, guard our path, and preserve our way. And third, *from above:* God will direct us into successful pursuits—righteousness, justice, equity, every good course—that give satisfaction (v. 9).

 ### Living Insights

We've thrown a lot of training and equipment at you in this last lesson, so let's pause before we proceed any further for a little evaluation. Perhaps this will help you gain a realistic picture of the strengths and weaknesses of your own mining skills. Under each excavating technique, mark the point on the line that best represents your level of ability.

I possess the right attitude toward God's Word.

Only on Sundays   Most Every Day

_____

I saturate my mind with God's Word.

Only on Sundays   Most Every Day

_____

I have an attentive ear.

Only on Sundays   Most Every Day

_____

I cultivate an open heart.

Only on Sundays   Most Every Day

_____

I proclaim the need for discernment.

Only on Sundays   Most Every Day

_____

I request understanding.

Only on Sundays   Most Every Day

_____

I seek wisdom with diligence.

Only on Sundays   Most Every Day

_____

I pursue wisdom with patience.

Only on Sundays   Most Every Day

_____

Living Insights STUDY TWO

Now that you've finished the evaluation, write a brief summary outlining what you see as your strengths and weaknesses. Include an explanation as to why you think you're stronger in some areas than others. Finally, make a proposal detailing what you can begin doing this week to realistically improve your efforts at prospecting for the gold of God's wisdom.

Summary

_____

_____

_____

_____

_____

_____

_____

_____

_____

_____

_____

Proposal

_____

_____

_____

_____

_____

_____

_____

_____

_____

Chapter 4

YOU AND YOUR SON
Selected Proverbs

S even years after the end of America's bloody Civil War, Josiah
Holland wrote,

> God, give us men! A time like this demands
> Strong minds, great hearts, true faith and ready
>   hands;
> Men whom the lust of office does not kill;
> Men whom the spoils of office cannot buy;
> Men who possess opinions and a will;
> Men who have honor; men who will not lie.[1]

It seems that the more times change, the more they stay essentially the same. For the call of that bygone era certainly rings
through our day as well.

God, give us men. Give us Noahs, to whom You can entrust
Your mighty plans; give us Abrahams, who are willing to leave
home and homeland to follow Your call; give us Josephs, who would
rather endure prison than violate one of Your commands; give us
Daniels, who would rather face a lions' den than compromise their
faith. *God, give us men.*

Before God gives us men, however, He gives us boys—boys
whom parents are to forge into men. To equip us for that task, the
Lord has provided us with some fatherly advice.

Five Areas of Teaching

From the wealth of Proverbs we can extract insight from at least
five areas of teaching that are essential if our sons are to grow up
to be honorable men of God.

This lesson was adapted from "You and Your Son" from the study guide *You and Your Child,*
coauthored by Lee Hough, from the Bible-teaching ministry of Charles R. Swindoll (Anaheim, Calif.: Insight for Living, 1993).

1. From Josiah Gilbert Holland's "God, Give Us Men!" in *The Best Loved Poems of the
American People,* comp. Hazel Felleman (Garden City, N.Y.: Garden City Publishing Co.,
1936), p. 132.

Teach Him to Stand Alone

Proverbs 1:10–19 highlights the need to teach our sons the importance of having biblical convictions and being willing to stand up for them—even when that means standing alone. Eugene Peterson's paraphrase is especially vivid:

> Dear friend, if bad companions tempt you,
>   don't go along with them.
> If they say—"Let's go out and raise some hell.
>   Let's beat up some old man, mug some old
>   woman.
> Let's pick them clean
>   and get them ready for their funerals.
> We'll load up on top-quality loot.
>   We'll haul it home by the truckload.
> Join us for the time of your life!
>   With us, it's share and share alike!"—
> Oh, friend, don't give them a second look;
>   don't listen to them for a minute.
> They're racing to a very bad end,
>   hurrying to ruin everything they lay hands on.
> Nobody robs a bank
>   with everyone watching,
> Yet that's what these people are doing—
>   they're doing themselves in.
> When you grab all you can get, that's what happens:
>   the more you get, the less you are.[2]

Essentially, Solomon is saying that if the crowd strays from God's path, then follow the path and not the crowd. Your child's peer group exerts a relentless pressure to conform and follow the pack. So if pointing out the right path isn't enough, perhaps a change in peer groups is necessary.

> He who walks with wise men will be wise,
> But the companion of fools will suffer harm.
> (13:20)

Changing friends is a painful and difficult experience, but parents can do at least two things to encourage their son to take that step

---

2. Eugene H. Peterson, *The Message: The Wisdom Books* (Colorado Springs, Colo.: NavPress, 1996), pp. 283–84.

on his own. First, *teach him what a good friend really is.* Write out a list of these qualities, and have him evaluate his present friendships in light of them. Then have him set his sights on the type of friends he would like to have. Second, *remind him of the consequences of wrong.* Psalm 73 does a good job of teaching us not to envy those who break the law but to consider the consequences of their actions.

> But as for me, my feet came close to stumbling;
> My steps had almost slipped.
> For I was envious of the arrogant,
> As I saw the prosperity of the wicked. . . .
> Until I came into the sanctuary of God;
> Then I perceived their end. . . .
> How they are destroyed in a moment!
> They are utterly swept away by sudden terrors! . . .
> For, behold, those who are far from Thee will perish.
> (vv. 2–3, 17, 19, 27a)

Since children are impressionable, showing the end result of wrong behavior is essential for them to be able to withstand the magnetic pull of their peer group.

Teach Him to Be Open to God's Counsel

Along with the ability to stand alone, our sons need to learn what is involved in being open to God's counsel and reproof. Proverbs 3:11–12 talks about this sensitivity to instruction.

> My son, do not reject the discipline of the Lord,
> Or loathe His reproof,
> For whom the Lord loves He reproves,
> Even as a father, the son in whom he delights.

A tender heart toward God is one of the hallmarks of true manhood. David, the great warrior who is described as being as fierce as "a bear robbed of her cubs" (2 Sam. 17:8), is also shown to be "a man after My heart, who will do all My will" (Acts 13:22).

How can we develop a sensitivity like David's in the lives of our sons? First of all, we need to teach him to respond to our counsel (compare Prov. 1:8–9; 3:1–4; 4:1–4; 7:1–3). If he treasures our counsel as a child, then treasuring God's counsel in his adulthood will be an easy transition.

Second, we must help him see the value of other people's correction. If he learns to respect the correction of his teachers, coaches, grandparents, and friends, it won't be so difficult to respond to God's discipline later on in his life.

Third, we should share the experiences of our life with him. Abstract principles are valuable, but lived-out lessons give our sons something firmer to hold on to, remember, and understand. Sharing our victories and defeats and what we've learned through them makes values more real.

Fourth, we've got to spend sufficient time counseling our sons. Forging great men for God takes time. Your presence and availability for your son will shape his personality for the full scope of life's responsibilities.

Teach Him How to Deal with Temptation

The two areas of temptation mentioned most in Proverbs come from the opposite sex and overindulgence in food and alcohol.

Sexual temptation. With regard to sexual temptation,[3] Proverbs 5:3–12 warns:

> For the lips of an adulteress drip honey,
> And smoother than oil is her speech;
> But in the end she is bitter as wormwood,
> Sharp as a two-edged sword.
> Her feet go down to death,
> Her steps lay hold of Sheol.
> She does not ponder the path of life;
> Her ways are unstable, she does not know it.
> Now then, my sons, listen to me,
> And do not depart from the words of my mouth.
> Keep your way far from her,
> And do not go near the door of her house,
> Lest you give your vigor to others,
> And your years to the cruel one;
> Lest strangers be filled with your strength,
> And your hard-earned goods go to the house of
>   an alien;
> And you groan at your latter end,

---

3. If your son is showing signs of struggling with homosexuality, we recommend the following resources: Michael R. Saia's book *Counseling the Homosexual* (Minneapolis, Minn.: Bethany House Publishers, 1988); Anita Worthen and Bob Davies' book *Someone I Love Is Gay: How Family and Friends Can Respond* (Downers Grove, Ill.: InterVarsity Press, 1996); and the ministry Exodus International, P.O. Box 77652, Seattle, WA 98177-0652; telephone (206) 784-7799.

When your flesh and your body are consumed;
And you say, "How I have hated instruction!
And my heart spurned reproof!"

We parents must extol the Edenic beauty of intimate marital love (see Song of Sol.; Prov. 5:15–19) and explain the dangers of the forbidden fruit of sexual relationships outside of marriage (5:20–23; 6:23–35; 7:4–27). As in Eden, temptation comes from the center of the garden—our hearts (compare Matt. 5:28). Whether your son resists lust or succumbs to it is determined on the daily battlefield of his heart.

To help prepare him for this battle, provide him with appropriate training concerning the development of his body and its normal, God-given drives. Also teach him how to detect even the slightest glimmer of immoral enticement—from outside sources or his own heart. Finally, instill in him the value of staying pure until marriage.

If our sons understand the depth of the meaning of sexual love; if they can successfully form healthy and emotionally intimate relationships; and if they can truly know that women are people of value made in God's image, not simply objects of pleasure—then they will have a greater chance of resisting temptation and avoiding the heartaches it holds . . . for themselves and others.

Temptation to overindulge. Proverbs also has some pointed advice with regard to food and drink:

> Listen, my son, and be wise,
> And direct your heart in the way.
> Do not be with heavy drinkers of wine,
> Or with gluttonous eaters of meat;
> For the heavy drinker and the glutton will come
>   to poverty,
> And drowsiness will clothe a man with rags.
> (Prov. 23:19–21)

Verses 29–35 are even more graphic and especially relevant in our day.

> Who has woe? Who has sorrow?
> Who has contentions? Who has complaining?
> Who has wounds without cause?
> Who has redness of eyes?
> Those who linger long over wine,
> Those who go to taste mixed wine.

Do not look on the wine when it is red,
When it sparkles in the cup,
When it goes down smoothly;
At the last it bites like a serpent,
And stings like a viper.
Your eyes will see strange things,
And your mind will utter perverse things.
And you will be like one who lies down in the
     middle of the sea,
Or like one who lies down on the top of a mast.
"They struck me, but I did not become ill;
They beat me, but I did not know it.
When shall I awake?
I will seek another drink."
(see also 20:1)

We need to be frank with our sons about the destruction that results from letting the search for pleasure dominate their lives. They need to know how easy it is to get hooked, how false the promises of lasting pleasure are, and how terribly difficult it is to free themselves from addiction's grip.

Teach Him How to Handle Money

We also need to teach our sons about the four basic areas of financial responsibility:[4]

- Giving: He should learn to honor the Lord with his income by making giving number one on his priority list (Prov. 3:9–10), especially giving to the poor (22:9).[5]

- Earning: In order to give, he must learn a skill with which he can derive an income (see Eph. 4:28; 1 Thess. 4:11; 2 Thess. 3:6–13).

- Spending: The woman in Proverbs 31 exemplifies how to wisely spend and invest money (see especially vv. 16, 24; compare Matt. 25:14–30).

---

4. An excellent resource for teaching your children how to handle money is *Money Matters for Parents and Their Kids*, by Ron and Judy Blue (Nashville, Tenn.: Thomas Nelson Publishers, Oliver Nelson, 1988).

5. God speaks very clearly and seriously about our treatment of the poor. For additional passages, see Proverbs 14:31; 17:5; 19:17; 21:13; 22:16, 22–23; 28:27; 29:7.

- Saving: Our sons must also learn the importance of providing not only for today but for tomorrow's needs too. Also, if they learn to save up for the things they want and need, they'll avoid the trap of deep credit card debt that has caught so many young people today (see Prov. 6:6–8).

Teach Him the Value of Hard Work

Two more passages from Proverbs underscore another important topic, the value of hard work.

> Poor is he who works with a negligent hand,
> But the hand of the diligent makes rich.
> He who gathers in summer is a son who acts
> wisely,
> But he who sleeps in harvest is a son who acts
> shamefully. . . .
> The soul of the sluggard craves and gets nothing,
> But the soul of the diligent is made fat.
> (Prov. 10:4–5; 13:4)

In a nutshell, hard work pays off. It is a grave mistake to give, give, give to a child without allowing him or her to experience the value and reward of hard, diligent work. Parents, give your children specific jobs to do around the home. Help them find ways of earning money and sharing in the expenses of their education. That will help prepare them for living on their own.

Two Added Ingredients

As you teach your son to be a man of God, you'll need two additional ingredients: *constant delight* and *consistent discipline*. While your son is learning the difficult lessons of discipline, he needs to know you care and delight in him so he won't be discouraged. Remember, everyone—including a child—learns more through positive, loving encouragement than a constant cascade of corrections.

 Living Insights STUDY ONE

How much do you really know about your parents' past?

What was your father like when he was a boy? What were your mother's adolescent years like? What did your parents struggle with?

Did they get along with their parents?

The sad fact is, many of us cannot answer even one of these questions. Our minds are blank when it comes to talking about our parents as people who were once children themselves. Will your son draw a blank too?

Sharing with our children about the ups and downs we experienced when we were their age is a powerful parenting tool.[6] It helps them see us as real people, not just distant authority figures. It also builds some important relational bridges, such as empathy and identification, between generations within the family. Bottom line, sharing your experiences will help your children be more open and relate to you better as you lead them through childhood and adolescence.

Why not use this study to help incorporate some personal sharing about your past? Now, we're *not* talking about those "When I was young, I used to walk five miles to school, barefoot, in the snow, both ways" kinds of stories. Save those for when the family goes fishing.

Do this instead: First, briefly share what Proverbs says about standing alone, for example. Then share how you learned about that from your parents. Or perhaps tell of a time when you didn't stand alone and what you regret about that. Rather than always hearing success stories, your children will appreciate knowing they're not the only ones in the family who have blown it in one of the five areas we've been studying. In fact, the result of sharing our shortcomings is usually that our children are more open about their own problems and about letting us know them on a deeper, more intimate level.

Spend some time reflecting on each of the five areas listed and see if they trigger any personal stories from your life or your parents' lives that you could share with your children.

Standing Alone _____

_____

_____

_____

6. For further study, read *The Power of Modeling* by Jorie Kincaid (Colorado Springs, Colo.: NavPress, 1989).

Being Open to God's Counsel _____

_____

_____

_____

Dealing with Temptation _____

_____

_____

_____

Handling Money _____

_____

_____

_____

Working Hard _____

_____

_____

_____

One last thing. Try sharing these types of stories at bedtime. No parent can hold a child's attention when it's play time and friends are calling. But when a child is in bed and not quite ready to sleep, you've got a captive audience—especially if there's humor involved. Like the time I didn't resist the temptation to make fun of my brother. I ended up hog-tied with my face covered in honey. But that wasn't the worst of it. Along came Happy, a honey-loving basset hound with enough drool to drown a person. . . . Want to hear the rest of that story?

Your kids will too.

Living Insights

As we draw this study to a close, consider one more verse from Proverbs that mentions the most important son ever born.

> Who has ascended into heaven and descended?
> Who has gathered the wind in His fists?
> Who has wrapped the waters in His garment?
> Who has established all the ends of the earth?
> What is His name or His son's name?
> Surely you know! (30:4)

Do you know that Son's name? Perhaps not. Perhaps you weren't given the kind of training presented in this study when you were young. Perhaps you were kicked around, ignored, resented, ill-treated, even despised. Strangely enough, so was this Son. Not by His parents, though, but by the very sons and daughters He created and for whom He came to give eternal life.

That Son's name, of course, is Jesus. He came to pay the penalty for your sins so that you could be reunited with your heavenly Father. Romans 6:23 says,

> For the wages of sin is death, but the free gift of God
> is eternal life in Christ Jesus our Lord.

If you've never placed your faith in Jesus Christ, you've missed the most important Son who's ever lived. We cannot make the kind of men out of our sons that the Scriptures teach until we first come to know God's Son for ourselves. How do we do that? According to John 3:16, it's by faith.

> "For God so loved the world, that He gave His only
> begotten Son, that whoever believes in Him should
> not perish, but have eternal life."

Raising a godly son begins with knowing the Son. Are you willing to begin knowing Him now?

Chapter 5

YOU AND YOUR DAUGHTER
(PART ONE)
Selected Proverbs

*G*one with the Wind, Margaret Mitchell's first and only novel, stands as a classic, both as a book and as a film. The backdrop to the story is the war-torn American South. But it's not so much a story about the Civil War. It's more a story about one woman— Scarlett O'Hara—a beguiling charmer whom men hovered over like bees on a blossom. However, under the coy twirl of the parasol that shaded her fine-china skin, beneath her rose-petal lips, behind the flirtatious flutter of her inviting eyes hid a heart of "snares and nets" (Eccles. 7:26).

For contrast, the author placed Scarlett beside the kind, selfless, tender Melanie. Next to her, Scarlett is seen for what she really is—a self-centered, manipulative, even ruthless woman.

In similar style, Proverbs often compares and contrasts its characters. We will compare and contrast two sets of women and, in doing so, learn about the qualities that can help our daughters become godly women.

The Foolish Woman versus the Wise Woman

Consider the two women in Proverbs 14:1.

> The wise woman builds her house,
> But the foolish tears it down with her own hands.

Let's examine each detail of the negative example first.

The Foolish Woman

Literally, the Hebrew word for *foolish* means "dull, thick, sluggish." The foolish woman is dulled to wisdom, calloused to correction, and sluggish in her response to God. Destruction lies in the wake of most every wave she makes.

The next phrase, *tears down*, means "to destroy," and it tells us something about this woman. She destroys her home and the people in it, dismantling them look by look, verbal jab by verbal jab, argument by argument until nothing is left. The tragic guilt of her actions is underscored by the emphatic phrase *with her own hands*. In the end, after years of troubling her own house, she will only "inherit wind" (11:29a).

No parents want a future like that for their little girl. But what many moms and dads fail to understand is that the foolish woman of Proverbs 14 started out as a foolish daughter—a daughter whose destructive bents were never fully recognized or effectively dealt with. So let's look at four diagnostic X rays of a foolish woman from Proverbs. Perhaps they will help us determine whether the condition exists in our daughters and what we can do to stop the malignancy before it spreads.

(1) *She is boisterous.* Notice the first sign in 9:13.

> The woman of folly is boisterous,
> She is naive, and knows nothing.

By *boisterous*, the text doesn't mean energetic or playful. Rather, the thought is one of commotion, rowdiness, loudness, and restlessness. In a parallel passage, Solomon links her boisterious quality with rebelliousness, which Eugene Peterson renders, "Brazen and brash she was, restless and roaming, never at home"[1] (7:11).

The chaos in her life is related to her being *naive* (9:13), a quality we sometimes equate with innocence and therefore admire. However, where innocence keeps one free and wholesome, naiveté leaves a girl wide open to danger through her lack of discernment and sound, informed judgment. Her thinking lacks the clarity to grasp the meaning of a situation and make a constructive choice. Her heart lacks the depth of understanding that would lead her turbulent soul toward a more peaceful path.

(2) *She makes a mockery of sin.* Proverbs 14:9a states: "Fools mock at sin." The foolish woman of chapter 9 illustrates this as she works at enticing an undiscerning man to adultery.

> "Stolen water is sweet;
> And bread eaten in secret is pleasant." (v. 17)

Her conscience is insensitive to sin, causing her to be flippant about morals and recklessly self-indulgent. Right and wrong are not important to her, only what is sweet and pleasant. Her live-for-the-

---

1. Eugene Peterson, *The Message: The Wisdom Books* (Colorado Springs, Colo.: NavPress, 1996), p. 294.

moment lifestyle is short-sighted, obscuring the long-term effects of her actions.

(3) *She is deceptive.* Proverbs 14:8b tells us that "the folly of fools is deceit." A foolish woman can look you eyeball-to-eyeball and, without batting a lash, lie to you in the most convincing way. The distinction between true and false vanishes into whatever is most convenient, and truth loses its meaning for her.

(4) *She is quarrelsome.* A final feature of foolishness appears in Proverbs 20:3.

> Keeping away from strife is an honor for a man,
> But any fool will quarrel.

The Hebrew term translated *quarrel* means to "*burst out* in contention, strife,"[2] which shows us that a foolish daughter would be argumentative and given to angry outbursts.

Now that you know what the symptoms of foolishness are, put your daughter behind the X-ray machine and take a good, hard look. Is she restless, tempestuous, racuous? Is sin "no big deal" to her, a joke? Is she deceitful and given to frequent lying? Does she look for a fight and try to start trouble?

If you see these symptoms in your daughter, the prognosis for her future is not good. In fact, we may say with a surgeon's frankness, her home will be like Scarlett's—troubled, torn down, and literally gone with the wind.

Equally bleak is the future of the foolish child's parents.

> He who begets a fool does so to his sorrow,
> And the father of a fool has no joy. (17:21)

However, parents who detect foolishness in their daughter early and deal with it decisively will grace the world with a Melanie—a wise woman who builds up her home.

But how exactly can parents help their children rid themselves of this deadly foolishness? Only one proverb actually describes the procedure:

> Foolishness is bound up in the heart of a child;
> The rod of discipline will remove it far from him.
> (22:15)

---

2. Francis Brown, S.R. Driver, and Charles A. Briggs, *The New Brown-Driver-Briggs-Gesenius Hebrew and English Lexicon* (Peabody, Mass.: Hendrickson Publishers, 1979) p. 166.

Coddling a child who is dull and insensitive, thick in his or her conscience, and who makes a mockery of guilt and sin only reinforces these tendencies. But consistent discipline applied with a physician's unflinching firmness and compassion will remove foolishness from the heart of a child. With his usual helpfulness, Dr. James Dobson gives parents practical advice on how to do this.

The overall objective during the preadolescent period is to teach the child that his actions have inevitable consequences. One of the most serious casualties in a permissive society is the failure to connect those two factors, behavior and consequences. Too often, a three-year-old child screams insults at his mother, but Mom stands blinking her eyes in confusion. A first grader launches an attack on his teacher, but the school makes allowances for his age and takes no action. . . . A fifteen-year-old sneaks the keys to the family car, but his father pays the fine when he is arrested. . . . You see, all through childhood, loving parents seem determined to intervene between behavior and consequences, breaking the connection and preventing the valuable learning that could have occurred. . . .

How does one connect behavior with consequences? By being willing to let the child experience a reasonable amount of pain or inconvenience when he behaves irresponsibly. When Jack misses the school bus through his own dawdling, let him walk a mile or two and enter school in midmorning (unless safety factors prevent this). If Janie carelessly loses her lunch money, let her skip a meal. Obviously, it is possible to carry this principle too far, being harsh and inflexible with an immature child. But the best approach is to expect boys and girls to carry the responsibility that is appropriate for their age, and occasionally to taste the bitter fruit that irresponsibility bears.[3]

3. James Dobson, *Dr. Dobson Answers Your Questions* (Wheaton, Ill.: Tyndale House Publishers, 1982), pp. 232–33.

The Wise Woman

In contrast to the foolish woman, "the wise woman builds her house" (14:1a). She's constructive instead of destructive. She establishes and maintains a strong, solid home. So how do parents raise their daughters to be such wise women? Proverbs 31 gives us five areas on which to concentrate.

First, *help her realize the value of being wise*.

> An excellent wife, who can find?
> For her worth is far above jewels. . . .
> She opens her mouth in wisdom,
> And the teaching of kindness is on her tongue.
> (vv. 10, 26)

When your daughter recognizes that wisdom is more precious than jewels (see 3:13–18), she will have taken the first step toward gaining that wisdom.

Second, *develop in her a caring spirit*. A wise woman has a servant's heart, investing herself in building up others.

> She rises also while it is still night,
> And gives food to her household,
> And portions to her maidens. . . .
> She extends her hand to the poor;
> And she stretches out her hands to the needy.
> (vv. 15, 20)

Your daughter is more likely to develop a sensitive, giving spirit if she sees the spirit of Christ incarnate in your everyday life (compare Mark 10:45; Phil. 2:3–8).

Third, *cultivate the skills of her hands*. This is the tangible expression of wisdom that helps her support and provide for herself.

> She looks for wool and flax,
> And works with her hands in delight.
> (Prov. 31:13)

Practical skills will serve her well throughout life as they foster her confidence and equip her to adeptly manage life's many responsibilities.

Fourth, *teach her how to handle money*.

> She considers a field and buys it;
> From her earnings she plants a vineyard. . . .
> She makes linen garments and sells them,

And supplies belts to the tradesmen.
(vv. 16, 24)

Girls need sound financial wisdom just as much as boys do. By opening up the world of money—teaching her to save, balance a checkbook, budget, avoid debt, invest, provide for retirement—you put in place priceless safeguards for your daughter's well-being. Ignorance and dependent helplessness in this area will not be the beauty marks of femininity; they will become the bruises of a person taken advantage of.[4]

Fifth, *open her eyes to the blessings of hard work.* A wise woman knows how to diligently apply herself to a task.

> She girds herself with strength,
> And makes her arms strong. . . .
> She stretches out her hands to the distaff,
> And her hands grasp the spindle. (vv. 17, 19)

And she will be rewarded by her efforts throughout her life:

> Strength and dignity are her clothing,
> And she smiles at the future. (v. 25)

Now that's what you want for your daughter, isn't it? By applying these five principles to your parenting, you will see your daughter develop strength and dignity . . . and a future to smile at.

The Contentious Woman versus the Gracious Woman

Another contrasting set of women in Proverbs is the contentious and the gracious woman. As before, let's examine the negative example first.

The Contentious Woman

Stand back and gaze at the disturbing portrait painted by the following verses from Proverbs.

> The contentions of a wife are a constant dripping.
> (19:13b)

---

4. An excellent resource for teaching your children how to handle money is *Money Matters for Parents and Their Kids,* by Ron and Judy Blue (Nashville, Tenn.: Thomas Nelson Publishers, 1988).

It is better to live in a corner of a roof,
Than in a house shared with a contentious woman.
(21:9)

It is better to live in a desert land,
Than with a contentious and vexing woman.
(v. 19)

A constant dripping on a day of steady rain
And a contentious woman are alike;
He who would restrain her restrains the wind,
And grasps oil with his right hand. (27:15–16)

Several images stand out in this picture. First, a leaky faucet. If you've ever had one keep you awake at night, you understand. Second, the corner of a roof. If you've ever been on your roof to fix an antenna, you know things would have to be pretty bad to consider living there. Third, a desert with blistering, relentless sun—doesn't sound too inviting, does it? Fourth, constant dripping on a rainy day, eroding your spirit drop by drop. And fifth, slippery oil. Try grabbing ahold of it sometime; it's frustratingly impossible.

All these images picture a woman given to strife. She thrives on stirring up conflict and unhappiness. And she always manages to get in the last word, the last jab. Like a continual drip . . . drip . . . drip, she drives you to the limits of your patience and sanity.

What causes a daughter to behave like this? An unchecked, stubborn will. Unless parents start early and work hard to develop a gracious, humble, teachable will in their daughter, Proverbs warns that "calamity will come suddenly; instantly [s]he will be broken, and there will be no healing" (6:15).[5]

The Gracious Woman

Fortunately, God gives us another picture to go by—the woman of Proverbs 11: "A gracious woman attains honor" (v. 16a). To be gracious means "to show favor." It is a picture of the person who is accepting and appreciative, thoughtful and considerate. This characteristic is most commonly used in reference to God:

The Lord is compassionate and gracious,
Slow to anger and abounding in lovingkindness.
(Ps. 103:8)

---

5. The story of Jezebel's death in 2 Kings 9:29–37 is an excellent example of this proverb.

Mirror graciousness to your daughter, clearly and consistently, and glimpse by glimpse she will become a changed person. Her words, appearance, and attitude will reflect the grace she sees in you. And someday, that daughter will grow to attain honor as a gracious woman.[6]

Living Insights

Now that we have compared and contrasted the wise woman and the foolish in Proverbs, let's compare and contrast the wise and foolish *influences* in our daughters' lives.

One of the primary influences is TV. James Dobson writes:

> By the time the average preschool child reaches fourteen years of age, he will have witnessed 18,000 murders on TV, and countless hours of related violence. . . . Dr. Saul Kapel states, furthermore, that the most time-consuming activity in the life of a child is neither school nor family interaction. It is television, absorbing 14,000 valuable hours during the course of childhood! That is equivalent to sitting before the tube eight hours a day, continuously for 4.9 years!
>
> . . . I am also concerned about the current fashion whereby each program director is compelled to include all the avant-garde ideas. . . . In recent seasons, for example, we were offered hilariously funny episodes involving abortion, divorce, extramarital relationships, rape, and the ever-popular theme, "Father is an idiot."[7]

According to an article in *Time* magazine, the average viewer sees more than 9,000 scenes of suggested sexual intercourse or innuendo on prime-time TV in one year.[8]

---

6. For additional help in teaching your daughter this Christlike characteristic, spend some time in the company of the Bible's wise and gracious women: Ruth, Hannah, Abigail, Esther, Mary (mother of Jesus), and Mary (Martha's sister).

7. Dobson, *Dr. Dobson Answers Your Questions*, p. 457.

8. Claudia Wallis, Cathy Booth, Melissa Ludtke, and Elizabeth Taylor, "Children Having Children," *Time*, December 9, 1985, p. 81.

Another major influence is advertising. Because teens spend and influence family spending to the tune of well over 150 billion dollars a year, the business and entertainment communities have tailored their advertising to exploit adolescent needs. In particular, they focus on the average teen's problem with self-esteem. By the time your daughter graduates from high school, she will have been bombarded by almost one million commercials telling her that she is something less than complete without a particular product.

But more than just products are being sold. Advertisers are selling images. Images of the rich and beautiful, sexy and popular, strong and powerful. And needy teenagers are buying. Time magazine noted, "Our young people . . . don't even buy toothpaste to clean their teeth. They buy it to be sexually attractive."[9] Influence? You bet.

What about the movie industry? According to Robert Coles, Harvard child psychologist and author of The Moral Life of Children, the values in today's movies are "hedonism, sexuality, violence, greed, selfishness."[10]

And what about music? "Violence, the occult, sadomasochism, rebellion, drug abuse, promiscuity, and homosexuality are constant themes," says U.S. News and World Report. Couple this with the fact that teens "listen to an estimated 10,500 hours of rock music between the seventh and 12th grades alone—just 500 hours less than the total time they spend in school over 12 years" and, well, you get the picture.[11]

Then, of course, there's the influence of peer pressure, MTV, magazines, pop stars, and the list goes on. Children are being swept away in a society that, like the fool in Psalm 14:1, believes that "there is no God."[12]

9. Wallis, Booth, Ludtke, and Taylor, "Children Having Children," p. 81.

10. As quoted by Steve Huntley and Harold R. Kennedy in "Expert Advice: Keep Control of Family Fun," U.S. News and World Report, October 28, 1985, p. 54. For further study, read Michael Medved's Hollywood vs. America: Popular Culture and the War on Traditional Values (New York, N.Y.: HarperCollins Publishers, Zondervan, 1992).

11. "What Entertainers Are Doing to Your Kids," U.S. News and World Report, October 28, 1985, p. 46. For a vivid example of music and its disturbed influence, read George Will's article "America's Slide into the Sewer" in Newsweek, July 30, 1990. The rap lyrics he discusses are graphic and shocking, but our society's tolerance and even endorsement of them are even more so.

12. See Focus on the Family's excellent video "A Generation at Risk," by Robert DeMoss, Jr., and their books Children at Risk: The Battle for the Hearts and Minds of Our Children, by James Dobson and Gary L. Bauer, and When Love Is Not Enough by Steve Arterburn and Jim Burns.

Now these things have not been mentioned so that everyone will burn their TV sets and stereos and go hide in the mountains. Rather, it's to give you just a sampling of the powerful influences toward foolishness your daughter must contend with daily.

Take time now to think about the *wise* influences your daughter is exposed to and list them in the space provided. For example, a Bible study; volunteer work; one-on-one time with Mom or Dad discussing current issues, films, or events from a Christian perspective; music or books with godly themes . . .

_____

_____

_____

_____

_____

_____

_____

_____

_____

_____

Last, if you do nothing to change the wise and foolish influences in your daughter's life right now, do you think she will grow to be a wise woman . . . or a foolish one?

Living Insights STUDY TWO

Read Proverbs 31:10–31 and note all the ways this woman exemplifies wisdom and grace.

_____

_____

_____

_____

_____

_____

_____

We know these traits don't naturally occur in children; they
have to be planted and watered by the parents. What do you think
the parents of the woman in Proverbs 31 did to cultivate these
kinds of traits in her?

_____

_____

_____

_____

_____

_____

_____

Of the things you listed, which are you doing for your daughter?

_____

_____

_____

_____

_____

_____

What, if anything, is lacking that you could focus on more?
How?

_____

_____

_____

Chapter 6

YOU AND YOUR DAUGHTER
(PART TWO)
Selected Proverbs

To continue the theme of our previous lesson, let's contrast two more pairs of women to find out which qualities need cultivating and which need culling in our daughters.

The Sensual Woman versus the Virtuous Woman

As before, let's begin our study of the opposites we find in Proverbs by examining the negative example first.

The Sensual Woman

Proverbs 2:16 describes the sexually promiscuous woman (the "adulteress") as *the strange woman*, which would be better rendered as "the estranged woman," because she is estranged from her family and alienated from the circle of proper relationships. Commentator Allen P. Ross adds that the strange woman is "outside the framework of the covenant community . . . with its social and religious conventions" prescribed by God.[1]

How can you detect signs of such a woman in your daughter? Proverbs provides us with five distinctive traits.

1. *By her words.* Proverbs 2:16 states that the sensual woman "flatters with her words," and 5:3 augments this picture:

> For the lips of an adulteress drip honey,
> And smoother than oil is her speech.

The daughter who is on her way to a life of promiscuity and ultimate emptiness depends on her ability to flatter and entice men instead of relating to them from the heart.

This lesson is adapted from "You and Your Daughter (Part Two)" from the study guide *You and Your Child*, coauthored by Lee Hough, from the Bible-teaching ministry of Charles R. Swindoll (Anaheim, Calif.: Insight for Living, 1993).

1. Allen P. Ross, "Proverbs," in *The Expositor's Bible Commentary*, gen. ed. Frank E. Gaebelein (Grand Rapids, Mich.: Zondervan Publishing House, 1991), vol. 5, p. 914.

2. *By her friends.* Notice our next clue in Proverbs 2:17a: she "leaves the companion of her youth." In this context, *companion* refers to the adulteress's husband. But in other passages, *companion* also means "friend," as in 13:20.

> He who walks with wise men will be wise.
> But the companion of fools will suffer harm.

Who are your daughter's companions—the wise or the foolish? Has she suddenly broken off her relationships with longtime friends? This will alert the wise parent to trouble—especially if the daughter begins to run with an older, faster crowd (see also 22:24–25; 1 Cor. 15:33).

3. *By her lack of spiritual commitment.* She "forgets the covenant of her God," according to Proverbs 2:17b. This shows up in the daughter who forsakes the spiritual truths she once held to embrace a worldly lifestyle.

4. *By her appearance.* Proverbs 7:10 says she dresses "as a harlot." In the Jewish culture of that day, prostitutes dressed in a fashion that made them easily identifiable. In our day, it's tough to distinguish that from just being fashionable. Some clues include how revealing the clothing is, whether it's designed to entice others rather than simply be attractive, and whether it does more to express the physical than convey the personality. Keep in touch with what's currently in style so you can really know this difference and avoid misjudging your daughter.

5. *By her attitude.* Proverbs 7:11–13a reveal her moods and behavior:

> She is boisterous and rebellious;
> Her feet do not remain at home;
> She is now in the streets, now in the squares,
> And lurks by every corner.
> So she seizes [a man] and kisses him.

In our last chapter, we learned that turbulence and tempestuousness mark the boisterous woman. Add to that the ideas of being disrespectful, hostile, fast, cunning, and aggressive, and you've got a pretty complete picture of an immoral, destructive woman's attitude.

Your daughter may never run off into the treacherous terrain of a sexually promiscuous life. However, she may be wandering precariously close to its borders if you can see some of these qualities emerging in her.

If you do see any similarities, take these warning signs to heart and plan some proactive steps. Studies have long shown that a growing daughter needs warmth, affection, and communication—especially from her father—if she is going to grow up healthy and whole. She needs smiles, hugs, and constant reassurances of your love. She needs candid talks on life, on what a man looks for in a woman, and on what the Bible says about inner and outer beauty (compare 1 Pet. 3:3–4).

Fathers, you can lose your daughters by default simply by not being there—or if there, by being silent and passive. Instead of taking a step back in rejection, take a step forward in acceptance and give her the biggest hug, the warmest smile, and the most sincere "I love you" that you possibly can. If you assure her of your love often enough, those messages will start transforming her from the inside out.

The Virtuous Woman

In stark contrast to all the ignoble qualities of the sensual woman are the excellent traits of the virtuous woman found in Proverbs 31. According to the Hebrew, *excellent* pictures strength and "efficiency." Such a woman is capable and has strength of character. She is also rare: "An excellent wife, who can find?" (v. 10a). She is someone of great value: "her worth is far above jewels" (v. 10b). And she is at the top of her husband's list: "Many daughters have done nobly, But you excel them all" (v. 29; see also 12:4).

The entire passage of Proverbs 31:10–31 holds this jewel of a woman up as a role model for every growing girl. Her finely cut facets sparkle brilliantly—she is trustworthy, diligent, capable, committed to her family's well-being, prudent, generous, strong, kind, has integrity, speaks wisely, and is appreciated by her family.

As a life assignment, begin using verses 10–31 as a prayer list for your daughter. It's the best way to get a diamond in the rough out of the rough!

The Indiscreet Woman versus the Godly Woman

In this, our final comparison, we'll learn that beauty is indeed only skin deep.

The Indiscreet Woman

A woman without discretion is depicted in ridiculous terms.

As a ring of gold in a swine's snout,
So is a beautiful woman who lacks discretion.
(Prov. 11:22)

The word *discretion* comes from the Hebrew word meaning "to taste," carrying the idea of discriminating taste (compare Ps. 34:8). It is the ability to choose between the tasteful and the tasteless, the appropriate and the inappropriate, right and wrong, good and bad. A woman lacking that ability, no matter how beautiful, becomes as repulsive as the runny snout of a pig. Her physical beauty, like the gold ring, is totally out of harmony with her inner self.

If your daughter is moving toward maturity with discretion, three things will be true. First, she will be able to perceive that which isn't obvious—she has discernment. Second, she will be able to interpret the unspoken—she can read between the lines. And third, she senses the implications of her actions and the actions of others—she knows choices have consequences, so she chooses carefully before she proceeds.

How do you instill such discretion in your daughter? By establishing biblical wisdom as the grid through which thought and behavior are filtered. God's Word is to be her—and your—frame of reference (see Ps. 119:66, 98–100). Also model discretion daily; don't wait until she's almost grown, then give her a crash course in character. Remember, too, dads, that this involves you as well as mom. Daughters need to know a man's views, struggles, thinking, and responses as well as a woman's.

The Godly Woman

In contrast to the disgusting image of the indiscreet woman is the pleasing picture of the godly woman in Proverbs 31:30.

Charm is deceitful and beauty is vain,
But a woman who fears the Lord, she shall be praised.

The woman who fears the Lord realizes that charm and elegance can conceal the truth of a woman's character and beauty can mask an empty life. She understands the need to cultivate an inner Christlike beauty that's eternal. For the daughter whose love for the Lord is the most obvious adornment of her life, praise will come, and she won't act indiscreetly in order to gain the attention of others.

Are we saying, then, that parents should teach their daughters to focus only on the inner person and ignore the outer one? Is dressing nicely and wearing jewelry wrong? No. The apostle Peter touches on this issue and provides some excellent advice to every young woman.

> And let not your adornment be *merely* external— braiding the hair, and wearing gold jewelry, or putting on dresses; but let it be the hidden person of the heart, with the imperishable quality of a gentle and quiet spirit, which is precious in the sight of God. (1 Pet. 3:3–4, emphasis added)

The source of genuine beauty for the Christian woman is her inner character. What she wears on the outside should be a nice complement to her inner spirit.

One of the greatest problems that your daughter will face growing up today, however, is the Madison Avenue message that physical beauty is everything for a woman. Almost every magazine, every commercial, every billboard, every movie communicates that message either explicitly or implicitly. And unless you get close enough to your daughter to model and affirm what is precious in God's sight, she may never get the true message . . . or know how truly precious she really is.

 Living Insights STUDY ONE

Mom and Dad, what is it that you affirm most often about your daughter? Is it her looks? Her musical ability? Her intelligence? Good manners? What about the traits of a virtuous and godly woman? When was the last time you praised your daughter for any of those?

Honestly, many of us have no answer for that last question. Such praise is really foreign to us. Sure, we take our daughters to church regularly, but then we fail to give them the continued spiritual encouragement they need at home. If only we could see how the precious blossoms of virtue and godliness wilt in our budding daughters simply for lack of nourishing praise.

Now some of you may be thinking,

> Must I brag on my child all day for every little thing [she] does? Isn't it possible to create a spoiled

brat by telling [her that her] every move is wonderful?[2]

Many parents have wondered about that same question. So many, in fact, that Dr. James Dobson included it in his best-seller *The New Dare to Discipline*. Listen to his wise response.

> Yes, inflationary praise is unwise. . . . [Your daughter] quickly catches on to your verbal game and your words then lose their meaning. It is helpful, therefore, to distinguish between the concepts of *flattery* and *praise*.
>
> Flattery is unearned. It is what Grandma says when she comes for a visit: "Oh, look at my beautiful little girl! You're getting prettier each day. I'll bet you'll have to beat the boys off with a club when you get to be a teenager!" . . . Flattery occurs when you heap compliments upon the child for something [she] does not achieve.
>
> Praise, on the other hand, is used to reinforce positive, constructive behavior. It should be highly specific rather than general. "You've been a good [girl] . . ." is unsatisfactory. "I like the way you kept your room clean today," is better. Parents should always watch for opportunities to offer genuine, well-deserved praise to their children, while avoiding empty flattery.[3]

Parents, nurture your daughter's godly traits with praise. To help you do this, use the following space to note the specific ways you've seen your daughter model virtue.

_____

_____

_____

_____

_____

2. James Dobson, *The New Dare to Discipline* (Wheaton, Ill.: Tyndale House Publishers, 1992), p. 96.

3. Dobson, *The New Dare to Discipline*, p. 96.

Now, on a separate sheet of paper, write your daughter a letter affirming the specific traits you've listed. It will be one of the most important letters you'll ever write, especially to her.

 Living Insights

This next assignment should give you some real living insights into your daughter!

Ask her to go out for a special evening with you—dinner, entertainment, the works. Be creative, and go out of your way to make it relaxed, memorable, and *fun*. No lectures. No correction. No parent-to-child talks. Nothing heavy or intimidating.

For one evening, forget you're an adult and try to get into her world. Music and movies are generally common ground with most children. Try not to pass judgment or offer any unsolicited opinions; instead, just listen and try to gain a broader understanding of your daughter.

It would be a treat for her if you shared what you were like when you were her age—how you felt about dating, your worst date, your best date, what movies and music were popular then, how you felt about growing up, how you felt about your parents, and so forth. Tailor the evening to her age and her interests.

Make it a scrapbook memory for her—and for you too—one you both will treasure for a lifetime.

Chapter 7
YOU AND YOUR TONGUE
Selected Proverbs

The story is told of a woman who complained to a venerated Puritan minister about the clerical bands he wore with his pulpit gown. Saying that they annoyed her greatly because they were too long, she then asked his permission to shorten them. The aged saint quietly acquiesced and handed her the offending bands. Armed with her scissors, the woman shortened the bands according to her tastes and then handed the fragments back to the minister. Unruffled, he thanked her and said, "Now, my good woman, there is something about you that is altogether too long that has annoyed me greatly. And since one good turn deserves another, I would like permission to shorten it."

"Certainly," she said, "you have my permission and here are the scissors."

Whereupon the wise pastor said, "Very well, madam, put out your tongue."[1]

We've all known people, like that woman, whose tongues needed trimming. A boss, maybe, or a neighbor, or perhaps even an in-law. But if we're honest, we'll have to admit that our own tongues have probably needed paring a time or two as well. We've all done it— held someone up in a conversation like a paper doll and snipped away until nothing was left but pieces on the floor. Am I right?

Very well, then . . . put out your tongue. No, no, no. Relax, I'm not suggesting we shorten it with scissors. I just want to have a look at it. That's it, stick it out there. Hmmm, just as the apostle James said. OK, you can put that little beast back in its cage behind your teeth now. I'm afraid the diagnosis isn't good for either you or me. Listen to what the Holy Spirit inspired James to write about the tongue two millennia ago.

> The tongue is a small part of the body, and yet it boasts of great things. Behold, how great a forest is set aflame by such a small fire! And the tongue is a

---

1. Adapted from Clarence Edward Macartney, *Macartney's Illustrations* (New York, N.Y.: Abingdon-Cokesbury Press, 1950), p. 396.

fire, the very world of iniquity; the tongue is set among our members as that which defiles the entire body, and sets on fire the course of our life, and is set on fire by hell. For every species of beasts and birds, of reptiles and creatures of the sea, is tamed, and has been tamed by the human race. But no one can tame the tongue; it is a restless evil and full of deadly poison. (3:5–8)

As you can tell, James feels strongly about the tongue, and his bedside manner in describing it is pretty blunt. But are we really supposed to believe that the two-ounce muscle in our mouths is the problem? No. In Luke 6:45, Jesus unmasks the real culprit.

"The good man out of the good treasure of his heart brings forth what is good; and the evil man out of the evil treasure brings forth what is evil; for his mouth speaks from that which fills his heart."

The tongue is actually neither friend nor foe. It's merely a messenger that delivers the dictates of the heart, either for good or evil. Wait . . . you may have read that last sentence too fast. Did you catch the part about the tongue being capable of *good* and not just evil? It's true. Solomon illustrated this important truth in Proverbs 15:2 by contrasting the words drawn from the wise and the foolish heart.

The tongue of the wise makes knowledge acceptable,
But the mouth of fools spouts folly.

For the rest of our time together in this lesson, let's consider four wise ways the tongue can be used for good. Then, in the next chapter, we'll examine some of the ways fools wag nothing but folly.

Right Uses of the Tongue

Using the tongue for good instead of evil is not something we all do automatically. We have to train ourselves by breaking bad habits and bridling our words to make them follow the paths of wise speech set forth in Proverbs. Let's travel down four of those paths for a closer look.

First: Wise Counsel, Sound Advice

The mouth of the righteous flows with wisdom. . . .
The lips of the wise spread knowledge. . . .

A wise man is he who listens to counsel.
(10:31a; 15:7a; 12:15b)

Life is full of difficult decisions that often leave us feeling overwhelmed, exasperated, and uncertain as to what we should do.
"Lord, just tell me where to go to college, who to marry, what career
to pursue, and where to live," we plead. But He doesn't typically
make those decisions for us in some supernatural way. Rather, He
helps us through the wise counsel of our godly friends and mentors.
Even Solomon, gifted as he was, still understood his own need, and
ours, for seeking counsel from others.

Oil and perfume make the heart glad,
So a man's counsel is sweet to his friend. . . .
Without consultation, plans are frustrated,
But with many counselors they succeed. (27:9; 15:22)

The next time a close friend has trouble clarifying the issues
surrounding a crossroads decision, make your companion's heart
glad with the sweet aroma of godly counsel.

Second: Reproof, Rebuke, Spiritual Exhortation

Another wise use of the tongue that's difficult for most to master
is found in 27:6.

Faithful are the wounds of a friend,
But deceitful are the kisses of an enemy.
(see also 27:17)

The value of a reproof shared in genuine humility and compassion is impossible to measure. If you've ever experienced such an
intimate exchange, you know that great insight and good are always
gained. Why? Primarily because the one who wounds does so out
of a deep love for the one being wounded. A true friend doesn't
rush to rebuke another, wielding his or her words "rashly like the
thrusts of a sword" (12:18a). People who delight in that kind of
reckless reproof know nothing of love. Their tongues haven't been
trained to bring healing, only hurt.

But the one who loves the other deeply rebukes reluctantly. He
or she does not delight in confrontation. They anguish over the
words that must be spoken. They pray with sweated brow for grace
and humility. They're going to bruise the one they love, and such
a duty is one of the most difficult and distasteful a friendship can

55

bear. Yet even though the bruise may linger, the pain will subside and the two will draw closer. To bear the coveted title of best friend, we sometimes must go through the painful rite of reproof.

Third: Encouragement

A third way to honor the Lord with our lips is beautifully expressed in 16:24.

> Pleasant words are a honeycomb,
> Sweet to the soul and healing to the bones.

The seeming simplicity of encouragement sometimes fails to catch our attention. We tend to underestimate the power of this unfeigned tool of the tongue. Yet for those who have experienced the sweet taste of sincere affirmation, nothing could be more exhilarating. Near miracles are wrought because of it.

> A well-timed word has the power to urge a runner to finish the race, to rekindle hope when despair has set in, to spark a bit of warmth in an otherwise cold life, to trigger healthful self-evaluation in someone who doesn't think much about his shortcomings, to renew confidence when problems have the upper hand.[2]

All because of the unobtrusive but effective use of approving words. Is there someone who has impacted your life in this way—perhaps a parent, teacher, mentor, or loyal friend? Have you ever stopped to thank them with a letter or a phone call? Maybe this is your opportunity to encourage them.

But don't stop there. Think about the people who are around you on a regular basis. Your friends at work or in school. How about your spouse, a secretary, an associate, the gardener, or your children? Do you ever take the time to jot a note or meet with them privately to express how much you genuinely appreciate them and why? Think about it.

Fourth: Witnessing, Teaching, Comforting

> The tongue of the righteous is as choice silver. . . .
> The teaching of the wise is a fountain of life,

---

2. Lawrence J. Crabb, Jr. and Dan B. Allender, *Encouragement: The Key to Caring* (Grand Rapids, Mich.: Zondervan Publishing House, 1984), p. 25.

To turn aside from the snares of death.
(10:20a; 13:14)

When we are born again, we automatically become ambassadors for Christ (see 2 Cor. 5:20). Each of us bears the tremendous responsibility of communicating God's truth by our words as well as our deeds (see Matt. 5:16). That means the way we use our tongues can impact others for eternity. Solomon wrote, "Death and life are in the power of the tongue" (Prov. 18:21a), and that is an incredibly sobering thought. Don't let it restrain you from witnessing, teaching, or comforting. Rather, let it serve as a constant reminder and encouragement to engage in these kinds of ministries, for they are truly the right uses of the tongue.

 Living Insights   STUDY ONE

Many of us are familiar with the name Larry Crabb. He's the author of several outstanding works in the field of counseling, such as *Basic Principles of Biblical Counseling*, *Effective Biblical Counseling*, and *Inside Out*. He's also written many other well-known books, like *The Marriage Builder* and *Finding God*. He holds a Ph.D. in clinical psychology from the University of Illinois and is the founder and director of the Institute of Biblical Counseling in Morrison, Colorado. In addition to being a counselor, writer, and teacher, this gifted communicator also conducts seminars around the country. His whole life is centered around speaking in one form or another. Who would've ever guessed that, growing up, this is the one thing he desperately wanted to avoid.

It seems Larry had a problem with stuttering when he was young. After a particularly humiliating experience in the ninth grade, he decided to shun all public speaking in the future. A short time later, however, he was pressured to pray in front of the congregation in his church. Listen to his memorable story.

> Filled less with worship than with nervousness, I found my theology becoming confused to the point of heresy. I remember thanking the Father for hanging on the cross and praising Christ for triumphantly bringing the Spirit from the grave. Stuttering throughout, I finally thought of the word Amen (perhaps the first evidence of the Spirit's leading), said it, and sat

down. I recall staring at the floor, too embarrassed to look around, and solemnly vowing never again to pray or speak aloud in front of a group. . . .

When the service was over, I darted toward the door, not wishing to encounter an elder who might feel obliged to correct my twisted theology. But I was not quick enough. An older Christian man named Jim Dunbar intercepted me, put his arm on my shoulder, and cleared his throat to speak.

I remember thinking to myself, "Here it comes. Oh well, just endure it and then get to the car." I then listened to this godly gentleman speak words that I can repeat verbatim today, more than twenty years later.

"Larry," he said, "there's one thing I want you to know. Whatever you do for the Lord, I'm behind you one thousand percent." Then he walked away.

Even as I write these words, my eyes fill with tears. I have yet to tell that story to an audience without at least mildly choking. Those words were life words. They had power. They reached deep into my being.[3]

God bless that man whose encouragement continues to directly benefit thousands through Larry Crabb's ministry today. Isn't that amazing? And yet, I bet if we were each to think back, we, too, could probably recall someone special who impacted our lives by their encouragement.

Who would that be for you? How have their words affected the course of your life?

_____

_____

_____

_____

We all hunger for "life words," as Larry put it. Most of us have tasted them before, but how much are we feeding others with them?

3. Crabb and Allender, *Encouragement: The Key to Caring*, pp. 24–25.

In the last week, whom have you made a conscious effort to encourage through a letter, a phone call, or a personal visit? Kind words cost us so little, yet why are we so miserly about giving them away?

Today, right now, spend some time in prayer asking God to sensitize you to those close to you who might need encouragement. As you pray, jot down whatever names come to mind and the kind of encouragement you sense they need.

_____

_____

_____

_____

 Living Insights

As you studied the lesson, did you sense the Holy Spirit's conviction in any particular one of the four good uses of the tongue? If so, write which use it was in the space provided.

_____

In what way were you convicted? Did you feel you should do more of something? Less? Was your thinking impacted in a way that made things more clear to you than ever before? Were you reminded of something you said recently that violated one of these principles? What?

This Living Insight isn't about doing what we want you to do, it's about listening and following the Holy Spirit's lead in what He wants you to do. If that's not clear yet, spend some time prayerfully rereading the passages where you felt His conviction. Ask Him to prompt within you the insight you need to understand His conviction and what to do about it. We'll leave you some space to record your thoughts.

_____

_____

_____

_____

Chapter 8

THE POISON IN YOUR MOUTH

Selected Proverbs

> But no one can tame the tongue; it is a restless evil and full of deadly poison. (James 3:8)

In his exposition of this verse, Guy King put the tongue's poison under the microscope of his focused study and made these important observations.

> The deadly drug does not need to be taken in large doses—a drop or two will suffice; and the tongue does not need to distil long speeches, it has but to drop a word, and the mischief is set afoot. Thus has a peace been ruined, thus has a reputation been blackened, thus has a friendship been embittered, thus has a mind been poisoned, thus has a life been blasted.[1]

So deadly can the tongue be that Jesus issued one of the sternest warnings in all of the New Testament concerning its use:

> "And I say to you, that every careless word that men shall speak, they shall render account for it in the day of judgment." (Matt. 12:36)

Sobering, isn't it? To think of all the things we said just yesterday that will be repeated before the judgment throne of God puts real panic in many of our hearts! And well it should. We're far too loose with our words. But what are some of those "careless words" that will one day come back to haunt us? Let's return to Proverbs for an uncomfortable look at the wrong ways we wag our tongues.

Wrong Uses of the Tongue

Spouting folly, to use Solomon's term (see Prov. 15:2), can take several unsavory forms.

---

1. Guy H. King, *A Belief That Behaves: An Expositional Study of the Epistle of James* (London, England: Marshall, Morgan and Scott, 1941), p. 63.

Deceitful Flattery

> A lying tongue hates those it crushes,
> And a flattering mouth works ruin. (26:28)

Two different ways to define flattery are (1) insincere compliments given to gain favor or (2) excessive, undue praise. Either way, Solomon warns us not to use it or be used by it.

> He who hates disguises it with his lips,
> But he lays up deceit in his heart.
> When he speaks graciously, do not believe him.
> (vv. 24–25a)

Our speech is to be marked by sincerity and truth, not hypocrisy and falsehood.

Slander, Talebearing, and Gossip

Another use of the tongue that concerned Solomon has to do with the malicious circulation of false or exaggerated reports about another person.

> He who spreads slander is a fool. . . .
> He who goes about as a talebearer reveals secrets,
> But he who is trustworthy conceals a matter.
> (10:18b; 11:13)

Even revealing the truth at times can be nothing more than a sneaky way to slander someone else. Private conversations aired publicly can cause irreparable damage. Not everything we hear should be shared. One who "repeats a matter," Solomon warns, "separates intimate friends" (17:9b).

But aren't there times when information ought to be given that may not seem kind? Yes. For example, Jesus' heated rebuke of the Pharisees recorded in Matthew 23. Seven times He denounced the hypocrisy of their puffed-up piety. It was a direct reproof done with the right motive—to correct wrong—not a case of vicious slander meant simply to hurt someone.

The topic of talebearing often raises another, more difficult, question: *Aren't there times when confidential information ought to be shared?* Again, the answer is yes. Not that it happens very often, mind you. But there are times when it becomes legally or morally necessary to break a trust. Say a friend admits that he's involved in an adulterous relationship; what do you do? According to Matthew 18:15–17, he should first be confronted privately. If that fails, then he's to be confronted by two or three witnesses. If that also fails, the whole church is to be told and disciplinary action taken (see also 1 Tim. 5:19–20).

Other examples of when a trust should be broken involve child abuse or times when someone's life is in danger. Clearly, in these types of cases, confidentiality must be broken in order to protect the innocent. Even so, only those who absolutely need to know should be told.

More often than not, the difficulty we face is not with breaking confidentiality but with keeping it. So how can we restrain our lips? By forcing ourselves to answer these four exacting questions before we unleash our tongues.

- Is it true? If you can't check the source, then don't share it.

- Is it confidential? If so, then keep it under lock and key.

- Is it kind? Will it build up another? If not, don't say it.

- Is it necessary? Does this other person need to know this? If it won't make any difference, it's usually best left unsaid.

Arguments, Strife, and Angry Words

Has someone ever verbally given you a black eye? Was it a sarcastic sucker punch that got you? I thought so. We've all received some cheap shots like that. Solomon took his share of hits from hot-tempered jabberers, and he had this to say about them:

> A fool's lips bring strife,
> And his mouth calls for blows.
> A fool's mouth is his ruin,
> And his lips are the snare of his soul.
> (Prov. 18:6–7)

Listen to the Living Bible's perception of this same person.

> A fool gets into constant fights. His mouth is his undoing! His words endanger him.

A little later in 29:22, Solomon again describes a brawler.

> An angry man stirs up strife,
> And a hot-tempered man abounds in transgression.
> (29:22)

What do you do when you're thrown in the ring with such a

person at work or in church or out in the community? The worst thing you can do is clench your tongue and start swinging. For a more practical way to protect yourself, read 17:14.

> The beginning of strife is like letting out water,
> So abandon the quarrel before it breaks out.

It takes two to fight. So, the moment you sense that's where a conversation is headed, walk away—don't get into the ring. Refuse to mix it up by trading verbal punches.

Another way to fend off fights is found in 22:24–25.

> Do not associate with a man given to anger;
> Or go with a hot-tempered man,
> Lest you learn his ways,
> And find a snare for yourself.

When you meet someone who blasts out anger in a stream of molten words—keep going! Don't pursue a relationship with this kind of person. Especially if you're single and this individual wants to go out with you. Can you imagine anything more foolish or painful than marrying an angry person who constantly abuses you with his or her two-fisted words?

Boasting and Foolish Talking

The fool feels compelled to comment on everything. Her words flow in an incessant cascade of bubbling babble that signifies nothing. He always jockeys for the coveted position of having the last word—and the first—and most everything in between.

But not the wise. You won't hear her filling the air with empty prattle. He has mastered the crucial skill found in 17:27–28.

> He who restrains his words has knowledge,
> And he who has a cool spirit is a man of understanding.
> Even a fool, when he keeps silent, is considered wise;
> When he closes his lips, he is counted prudent.

Solomon depicts the folly of those who don't restrain their words in several different ways. For example, foolish jesting:

> He who mocks the poor reproaches his Maker;
> He who rejoices at calamity will not go unpunished.
> (17:5)

These days, many of the best-known comedians, male and female, constantly tell sick jokes about the misfortunes of others. They love to make us howl about adultery, poverty, murder, and perversion. And the truly sick part is, we're laughing.

A second trait of the fool is impulsiveness.

> He who gives an answer before he hears,
> It is folly and shame to him. (18:13)

Have you ever done this before? Somebody starts to make a point, and before he or she can finish, you jump in with both feet and start kicking and screaming to defend yourself. But when you finally quit fighting and listen to the rest of the story, you realize all you've done is stick both feet in your mouth? Embarrassing, wasn't it?

A third way we talk too much is with our boasting.

> Like clouds and wind without rain
> Is a man who boasts of his gifts falsely. (25:14)

The simplest way to avoid this mistake is to refrain from boasting altogether. Follow, instead, Solomon's advice:

> Let another praise you, and not your own mouth;
> A stranger, and not your own lips. (27:2)

Profanity and Vulgarity

Today, the airwaves are polluted with profanity. Television flaunts sexual immorality and innuendo. Hollywood continues to assault us with its nefarious penchant for pornography. Everywhere around us we see and hear this kind of crude folly. But this isn't simply the world's problem. Many Christians seem to have trouble breaking profane habits from their past. Far too many of us curse and laugh at lewd jokes, making our witness perhaps the biggest joke of all.

Perversion in the tongue, Solomon says, "crushes the spirit" (15:4). Maybe you grew up with a parent who cursed. Or perhaps you're working for someone now whose every other word is a mindless, obscene oath. It wears you down, doesn't it? You just get sick of hearing the filth that stains your memory, leaving you feeling unclean.

Unfortunately, the "kind of man whose teeth are like swords, And his jaw teeth like knives" (30:14a) is common in politics, sports, the military, among blue collar workers, business professionals, the entertainment industry, church softball leagues, and just about anywhere else you could name.

To the wise person, cursing is neither attractive nor fitting. It is juvenile and ugly; a pitifully base way to express ourselves. We have a choice, remember. "Death and life are in the power of the tongue" (18:21). Which are you wielding?

Lies and Exaggerations

The last wrong use of the tongue is found in Proverbs 6:16–19.

> There are six things which the Lord hates,
> Yes, seven which are an abomination to Him:
> Haughty eyes, a lying tongue,
> And hands that shed innocent blood,
> A heart that devises wicked plans,
> Feet that run rapidly to evil,
> A false witness who utters lies,
> And one who spreads strife among brothers.

Notice that out of the seven abominations the Lord hates, the tongue is mentioned three times. And twice specifically for lying! That *really* bothers our holy Father. So why doesn't it bother us as well? Why are we so lax about telling the truth, the whole truth, and nothing but the truth? Why is it that today a Christian's word is viewed with laughable contempt in many circles? It's because we've forgotten what it means to be holy, and we've adopted the relative values of the world we live in. So we lie, we fail to keep our word, we exaggerate, we try to cover up. But as Solomon warns us, and as experience has all too painfully proven,

> A false witness will not go unpunished,
> And he who tells lies will not escape. (19:5)

What could be more damning to our witness as bearers of the truth than our own lies? Speak the truth, practice it, handle it accurately. Remember that your word is a reflection not only of your character, but also of God's.

 Living Insights

Flattery—Slander—Strife—Boasting—Profanity—Lies
This is one sinister line-up of lawless words! Take a good look at each one. Do you recognize any of these rogues in yourself? See

if you can identify the one verbal offender people are most likely to hear from your lips.

In a way, you've just signed a confession. Now, the law requires that you should be read your rights and booked. "You have the right to remain silent. Anything you say can and will be used against you." But this isn't a bust, so you needn't start worrying about bail. Besides, someone has already paid the "Wrongful Use" fine for your tongue long ago, so you're free to go.

That someone, of course, is Jesus (2 Cor. 5:21). Take a moment to thank Him, and then let's consider some specific steps to keep you out of trouble with this particular use of the tongue.

◆

Remember the four questions we recommended to interrogate your thoughts before they're released?

1. Is it true?
2. Is it confidential?
3. Is it kind?
4. Is it necessary?

I want you to think of the person or place that habitually tempts you to use your tongue in the way you confessed earlier. Got it? Now, what's the first thing you can do to break this cycle so that you're not a repeat offender? No, it doesn't have anything to do with the questions—not yet. Think back to what Solomon said in Proverbs 22:24–25. Then read 1 Corinthians 15:33.

Apply what you've just read to your situation. Do you need to stop associating with someone who's a bad influence? Is there a particular place you should avoid? That's the first step to consider.

But let's say you can't avoid a particular person or place. Maybe it's someone you work beside or carpool with or live next to. Now use the questions. You've got to consciously, carefully begin to control the flow of your words by testing them first to see whether they are true, confidential, kind, or necessary.

Are you willing to put forth that effort? I think you'll be amazed at how much and how quickly these questions can help. Set aside a few minutes to take this matter before the Lord. Ask Him for a sensitivity to know when to apply those criteria and how. Then, in the space provided, keep track over the next few days of the different ways this helps your tongue talk the straight and narrow.

_____

_____

_____

_____

_____

_____

 Living Insights

My friend Rob Moore probably doesn't even remember the conversation. I'll never forget it.

It was years ago, before either one of us was married. We were rooming together, and I stopped him one day to talk about something I'd heard about someone else.

"Did you hear about . . . ?" I shared the news with my best "concerned Christian" face, but the truth is, I wasn't all that genuinely concerned. I was simply enjoying the smug satisfaction that comes from revealing all the illicit tidbits about someone else's mistakes. Right down to the last detail.

Rob listened patiently and then asked one question. *"How do you know that's true?"* The words left me speechless. Why? Because I suddenly realized that I didn't know if the story was true. I had no idea. Yet I had just related it to him as if it were.

About the only thing that was true in that embarrassing moment was my own hypocrisy. I hadn't been the least bit concerned with the accuracy of the story or, really, the person it was about. Gossip—guilty. Slander—guilty. Exaggeration—guilty.

Thanks, Rob Moore. I haven't forgotten the lesson you taught me. It has kept me from falling into the trap of gossiping about others countless times.

It could do the same for you if you'll ask yourself that same, unflinching question each time you're tempted to talk about someone else . . .

How do you know that's true?

Chapter 9

YOU AND YOUR JOB
(PART ONE)
Selected Proverbs

D o you do your best at work? Pursuing excellence is a rare commodity among many Americans today. Even rarer, it seems, and more disconcerting, is the number of Christians who actually do quality work. Our witness on the assembly line and in the office has become so disreputable that many personnel directors and presidents are now saying that they prefer *not* to hire Christians.

How many of you have felt that same disgust and distrust? How many times has it been the "trust me I'm a Christian," not the non-Christian, who has gone back on his or her word to you in business? Or defaulted on a debt? Or lied about the work that was done? Too many times, I suspect. And, undoubtedly, some of the individuals who ripped you off still proudly serve as deacons and elders in their churches.

This outrageous slandering of the name of Christ must be stopped! Could you imagine Moses shortchanging the shearers so he could have a little extra spending money for his return trip to Egypt? And what about Paul? Tent making was his trade. Is it likely he billed his clients for hours he never worked and then went out to tell people "Jesus saves"? Jesus was a carpenter. Do you think He was lazy? "I'm going to quit when I'm thirty anyway, so why bother?" Did He cut corners on quality and pass it off as "just business"? Of course not. Our work, like everything else, is a reflection of who we are and of the truth we proclaim. "Whatever you do," Paul wrote,

> do your work heartily, as for the Lord rather than for men; knowing that from the Lord you will receive the reward of the inheritance. It is the Lord Christ whom you serve. (Col. 3:23–24)

What's happened to that kind of work ethic among Christians? Why have we forsaken God's high calling to work hard? Perhaps it's time we took a close look at ourselves as employees in the mirror of Proverbs. In this lesson and the next, let's inspect the work force Solomon portrays to see if the habits and attitudes he's describing are our own.

Employees Nobody Wants

The initial group we'll interview consists of three undesirables no one wants to hire. Unfortunately, our first candidate canceled at the last moment—said something rather strange about a lion lurking near his home. But let's have a look at his qualifications anyway.

The Sluggard

> I passed by the field of the sluggard,
> And by the vineyard of the man lacking sense;
> And behold, it was completely overgrown with
>   thistles,
> Its surface was covered with nettles,
> And its stone wall was broken down.
> When I saw, I reflected upon it;
> I looked, and received instruction.
> "A little sleep, a little slumber,
> A little folding of the hands to rest,"
> Then your poverty will come as a robber,
> And your want like an armed man.
> (Prov. 24:30–34)

Sluggards come in all shapes and sizes—and denominations. Despite whatever creed they may claim, laziness is the only real on-the-job doctrine they vigorously practice. Each day they repeat the complainer's liturgy, which goes something like this: "What time is it? It's not my job. What time is it? I don't get paid enough to do this. What time is it—is it five o'clock yet?"

Beyond being a whiner, the sluggard is characterized by six other telltale signs.

1. *He has trouble getting started.*

> How long will you lie down, O sluggard?
> When will you arise from your sleep? (6:9)

Notice the two questions: *how long* and *when*. Couch potatoes who live by the motto "Never do today what you can put off until tomorrow" hate such pesky questions. Sure, they can tell you when all their favorite game shows begin, but tell you when they're going to start working on that leaky faucet they promised to fix? "Soon, real soon. I just need a little more rest . . . ZZZZZZZZZZZz" (v. 10).

2. *She is restless—filled with inner plans she never implements.*

The soul of the sluggard craves and gets nothing,
But the soul of the diligent is made fat. . . .
The desire of the sluggard puts him to death,
For his hands refuse to work. (13:4; 21:25)

No clearer example of this can be found than in the life of Samuel Taylor Coleridge.

> Never did so great a mind produce so little. He left Cambridge University to join the army; he left the army because, in spite of all his erudition, he could not rub down a horse; he returned to Oxford and left without a degree. He began a paper called *The Watchman* which lived for ten numbers and then died. It has been said of him: "He lost himself in visions of work to be done, that always remained to be done. Coleridge had every poetic gift but one— the gift of sustained and concentrated effort." In his head and in his mind he had all kinds of books, as he said, himself, "completed save for transcription." . . . But the books were never composed outside Coleridge's mind, because he would not face the discipline of sitting down to write them out.[1]

"For his hands refused to work"—a poignant epitaph for a disappointing life.

3. *He is costly to the business.*

> He also who is slack in his work
> Is brother to him who destroys. (18:9)

Sluggards don't actually go around destroying things—they're too lazy for something so physically strenuous. But they do know how to destroy office morale with deadly gossip and how to turn profit into loss through slow productivity.

4. *She is often very defensive.*

> The sluggard is wiser in his own eyes
> Than seven men who can give a discreet answer.
> (26:16)

1. William Barclay, *The Gospel of Matthew*, vol. 1, rev. ed., The Daily Study Bible Series (Philadelphia, Pa.: Westminster Press, 1975), p. 280.

You'll never see a sluggard so animated as when she attempts to defend herself when confronted. Suddenly she's a paragon of virtue and industry, always right, always ready with a reason for everything, and deeply offended that you would dare question her work habits. Shame on you!

5. *He is a quitter.*

> A slothful man does not roast his prey,
> But the precious possession of a man is diligence.
> (12:27)

For you nonhunter types, the truth behind this proverb may seem about as clear as a deer in a thicket. What Solomon means is that the sluggard is too lazy to cook the game he kills. He may like to fish, for example, but he hates cleaning the catch. He starts out in all his endeavors with lots of enthusiasm, but then he fizzles for a nap before the work is finished.

6. *She lives under self-delusional excuses.*

> The sluggard says, "There is a lion outside;
> I shall be slain in the streets!" (22:13)

This is not your ordinary "I can't come in today, I'm sick" kind of excuse. Oh no. That's too banal for the self-respecting sluggard. The ancient lion-in-the-street ploy is melodramatic excuse making raised to an art form. And that's just what it is for most sluggards, who have a way of channeling all their creative energies into making excuses instead of a living.

Ah, Mr. Sluggard, what a surprise. I see you braved the lion to make it here after all. We just finished examining your résumé, and I'm afraid we don't have any openings right now (or ever) for someone with your particular qualifications. If I may, however, I'd like to offer you two words of advice that may help you in the future. The first is found in Proverbs 6:6–8.

> Go to the ant, O sluggard,
> Observe her ways and be wise,
> Which, having no chief,
> Officer or ruler,
> Prepares her food in the summer,
> And gathers her provision in the harvest.

Remember the object lesson of the ant. It needs no boss to check up on it. It works hard in spite of the difficulties. And it plans ahead for the hard times. A wonderful example for you to emulate.

My second counsel is a word of warning. Remember, if you continue to fold your hands for "a little sleep, a little slumber," Solomon has said that "your poverty will come in like a vagabond, And your need like an armed man" (vv. 10–11).

The Deceiver

Solomon gives us a glimpse of our next interviewee in 11:18, a smooth, sweet-talking type:

> The wicked earns deceptive wages,
> But he who sows righteousness gets a true reward.

This is the employee who typically whispers things like, "No one will ever know," "Don't worry about it, everybody does it," and, "This is smart business. Besides, they owe it to me after all the hard work I've put into this company."

Have you ever worked with a deceiver before? Or maybe been conned by one wearing an *ichthus*[2] symbol and a "trust me, Brother" smile? I thought so. Most of us have, so let's see what helpful insights Solomon can give us about this worker of deceit.

1. *He appears to have a life of ease, but it's really empty and without purpose.*

> Wealth obtained by fraud dwindles. (13:11a)

The meaning of the Hebrew term for *wealth* has to do with more than just money. It also refers to what's "necessary to make life 'easy.'"[3] So it's the deceiver's "ease of life" that dwindles as his fraudulent activity continues. This same truth is reaffirmed a little later in 15:27a: "He who profits illicitly troubles his own house."

2. *The deception may be exciting initially, but its end is bitter and hard to bear.*

> Bread obtained by falsehood is sweet to a man,
> But afterward his mouth will be filled with gravel.
> (20:17)

2. An *ichthus* is "a representation of a fish used in ancient times . . . as a Christian symbol for the Greek word *ichthys* interpreted as an acrostic in which the Greek letters are the initials of the words Iesous Christos theou hyios sōtēr meaning Jesus Christ Son of God Savior." See *Webster's Third New International Dictionary of the English Language Unabridged* (Springfield, Mass.: Merriam-Webster, Inc.), 1981, p. 1121.

3. R. Laird Harris, Gleason L. Archer, Jr., and Bruce K. Waltke, eds., *Theological Wordbook of the Old Testament* (Chicago, Ill.: Moody Press, 1980), vol. 1, p. 213.

Don't let anyone tell you that sin doesn't exhilarate. It does. Successfully stealing something produces a twisted kind of "high." You feel cocky and lucky and excited all at the same time. And it's not only the professional thief who experiences such feelings; it's everyone who steals, from the office worker who pilfers pens and paper clips to the president who siphons off thousands every year. Like all emotions, however, that fugitive feeling soon steals away, leaving in its place the gritty taste of reality—guilt, shame, and a deadness of spirit.

Do you pay for everything you take home from your job?

3. *He lacks a sense of loyalty.*

> Like a bad tooth and an unsteady foot
> Is confidence in a faithless man in time of
>   trouble. (25:19)

The deceiver is also disloyal. You can't count on him. He'll be one of the first to abandon ship and leave you stranded when hard times hit.

You can come in now, Mr. Deceiver. I've examined your résumé and—pardon me? Oh, thank you. I've always liked this tie too. As I was saying—excuse me? Yes, I noticed the *ichthus* on your lapel. If I could just—you mentored Francis Schaeffer? Amazing. Even so, "Brother," I'm afraid your talents just don't fit the needs of this company. Perhaps if you were to follow Paul's advice in Ephesians 4:28, you'd keep your next job and never have to apply for another.

> Let him who steals steal no longer; but rather let
> him labor, performing with his own hands what is
> good, in order that he may have something to share
> with him who has need.

The Greedy

Our last applicant to review is presented to us in Proverbs 28:22.

> A man with an evil eye hastens after wealth,
> And does not know that want will come upon
>   him.

People who chase after riches say things like, "When I make my first million . . . " and, "All I need is just a little bit more, and then I'll quit, I promise." Of course, they never do. Work is number one for these people. Marriage, family, serving others—none of these matter as much as making a buck. But that's not all. Let's dig a little deeper into this person's background by reading still more from Solomon's personnel files in Proverbs.

1. *He attempts to find security in money.*

> He who trusts in his riches will fall,
> But the righteous will flourish like the green leaf.
> (11:28)

Money satisfies. It holds the key to real happiness. Or so the greedy believe with religious fervor. But they worship a paper god that can never give what the priests of marketing promise (see Eccles. 5:10).

2. *She never slows her fanatical pursuit of riches.*

> Do not weary yourself to gain wealth,
> Cease from your consideration of it.
> When you set your eyes on it, it is gone.
> For wealth certainly makes itself wings,
> Like an eagle that flies toward the heavens.
> (Prov. 23:4–5)

Despite all promises and warnings, the greedy often refuse to abandon their quest for the pot of gold at the end of the rainbow. Even those who obtain the riches they set out to find soon discover that, instead of lasting satisfaction and joy, they now feel a new discontent that drives them to work even harder and make even more.

3. *He is extremely selfish.* Jesus pictured this aspect of the greedy person in a parable.

> "The land of a certain rich man was very productive. And he began reasoning to himself, saying, 'What shall I do, since I have no place to store my crops?' And he said, 'This is what I will do: I will tear down my barns, and build larger ones, and there I will store all my grain and my goods. And I will say to my soul, "Soul, you have many goods laid up for many years to come; take your ease, eat, drink and be merry."' But God said to him, 'You fool! This very night your soul is required of you; and now who will own what you have prepared?'" . . . And [Jesus] said to them, "Beware, and be on your guard against every form of greed; for not even when one

74

has an abundance does his life consist of his possessions." (Luke 12:16–20, 15)

Like the rich man, all greedy individuals measure their lives by
the treasures they hoard. Selfishness consumes their every motive,
act, and relationship.

4. *She will get burned because of her greed.*

> A faithful man will abound with blessings,
> But he who makes haste to be rich will not go
> unpunished. (Prov. 28:20)

Greed rewards its followers with loneliness, broken marriages,
alienated children, lots of enemies, drug abuse, emptiness, prison,
and, at times, even suicide.

Well, I think that tells us all we need to know about this kind
of employee. I'm sorry, Mr. Greedy, but I'm afraid we won't be able
to hire you, either. Let me encourage you to read the *entire* book
of Ecclesiastes. It was written by a wealthy individual I'm sure you'll
admire, whose advice may help you rethink some of your financial
goals. Perhaps then you could come back and we'll reconsider your
application. Oh, I see . . . you think God can best use a humble
servant like yourself ministering to the rich.

Uh-oh!

 Living Insights STUDY ONE

As you looked in Solomon's mirror at the sluggard, the deceiver,
and the greedy, did any of what you saw reflect the way you behave
as an employee? For far too many Christians, the likeness is
uncomfortably accurate. Why? What makes our witness at work
resemble one of those three characters instead of Christ?

In their excellent book *Your Work Matters to God*, authors Doug
Sherman and William Hendricks answer that question with this
important insight.

> At the beginning of creation, work may have started
> out in a garden. But in our generation it has ended
> up in a jungle. . . .
> . . . Work has become warlike, as workers seek
> competitive advantage over others. To survive and
> prevail requires "intimidating friends and seducing

people." Consequently, distractions such as moral scruples must be left behind when one enters the jungle. A sort of moral Darwinism rules there: Survival depends on doing not what is right, but what works.

. . . In such a jungle, it seems predictable that [the worker] will do *whatever* it takes to achieve his goals:

> What is good is what one finds rewarding. If one's preferences change, so does the nature of the good. Even the deepest ethical virtues are justified as matters of personal preference. Indeed, the ultimate ethical rule is simply that individuals should be able to pursue whatever they find rewarding, constrained only by the requirement that they not interfere with the "value systems" of others. [Bellah, et al., *Habits of the Heart*, p. 6]

This nullifies lasting commitment to anyone or anything outside of oneself. If a relationship (spouse, child, friend, subordinate) stands in the way, one sacrifices it. If a boss or board obstructs one's progress, one goes to work undercover. If legal or moral issues prove bothersome, one compromises them. All on the basis of expediency.

Such a principle is purely secular in that the individual himself not only sets his goals, but sets his rules as well. He sees no authority or value system higher than himself to which he will ultimately submit.[4]

Even Christians? Yes, even Christians. We have forgotten Paul's admonition that it is the Lord Christ whom we serve, not expediency. Somehow we have separated our work from the reach of God's rules, and we play by the laws of the jungle instead. That's why the world often can't discern any difference between the Christian and the non-Christian in the workplace.

Is your behavior on the job governed by what works instead of by what's right? Do you do whatever it takes to get results, even if that means bending the truth or breaking a few rules?

---

4. Doug Sherman and William Hendricks, *Your Work Matters to God* (Colorado Springs, Colo.: NavPress, 1987), pp. 31–32.

"But that's just business. Everybody does it." Hmmm. Now where have we heard that before?

 Living Insights

This may hurt a little.

Now I realize none of us likes having to admit to weaknesses or mistakes. And I also know that it would be a lot more fun to just sit back and criticize those three workers from the lesson. But that's not the shot in the arm we need to correct some of our own mistakes. To do that we've got to painstakingly examine ourselves in the light of the characteristics we noted about the sluggard, the deceiver, and the greedy.

If it will make you feel any better, I'll go first.

Do I have trouble getting started?

Sometimes I do have trouble getting started. It seems to happen most when several big things stack up on me all at the same time. I start feeling overwhelmed, and then do you know what I do? "A little sleep, a little slumber, a little folding of the hands." That's right, I rack out. I just shut the world out and hibernate.

There now, that wasn't so bad. Now it's your turn. Look through each of the characteristics and jot down any of your own weaknesses.

_____

_____

_____

Am I restless—filled with inner plans I never implement?

_____

_____

_____

Am I costly to my business?

_____

_____

_____

Am I often defensive?

_____

_____

_____

Am I a quitter?

_____

_____

_____

Do I constantly make excuses for my sloppy work?

_____

_____

_____

Do I lack a sense of loyalty?

_____

_____

_____

Am I attempting to find security in money?

_____

_____

_____

*Am I extremely self-centered about the way
I spend and seek to earn more money?*

_____

_____

_____

Finally, what counsel have you gleaned from Proverbs or elsewhere that can help you improve?

For me, I'm learning how to break down big problems into bite-sized chunks. That way I get started quicker without experiencing sleepiness brought on by acute panic!

_____

_____

_____

_____

_____

Chapter 10

YOU AND YOUR JOB
(PART TWO)
Selected Proverbs

Next!

We're ready to begin our second round of interviews, drawing once again from the pool of applicants in Proverbs. This time, however, our focus will be on the *right* kind of worker.

Employees Everybody Wants

Fortunately, not all Christians are sluggards, deceivers, or greed-mongers. Many do their work heartily as unto the Lord, leaving behind on every job an unmistakable calling card about their character and their God. We're about to meet three such respected workers. Ah, here comes the first one . . . right on time as usual.

The Diligent

Please, come in and have a seat. Let's look at the qualifications Solomon lists about you.

> Poor is he who works with a negligent hand,
> But the hand of the diligent makes rich. (Prov. 10:4)

The Hebrew term for *diligent* can mean "to cut or sharpen." It's used here to connote the kind of worker who is sharp, decisive, keen—three impressive traits that would grab any employer's attention. Adding to these, Solomon gives four other outstanding recommendations.

1. *He shows discipline and determination.* Both of these qualities are readily visible in the diligent. He is steady, earnest, and enthusiastic. He knows how to avoid distractions and make good use of his time. You can depend on him to handle situations with efficiency. He accomplishes his goals.

2. *She demonstrates an alert awareness.* This, too, is implied by the Hebrew term for *diligent* in verse 4. She is perceptive, on top of things, able to anticipate what to do without having to be told every step of the way.

3. *He is a rare and valuable find.*

> A slothful man does not roast his prey,
> But the precious possession of a man is diligence.
> (12:27)

The term for *precious* suggests rarity. Diligent workers are as rare a find in the workplace as precious gems are in nature. Employers must usually dig at considerable cost to uncover an individual whose performance shines with this prized quality.

4. *She is a reservoir of plans and ideas.*

> The plans of the diligent lead surely to
> advantage,
> But everyone who is hasty comes surely to
> poverty. (21:5)

According to the *Theological Wordbook of the Old Testament*, the basic idea of the word *plans* is "the employment of the mind in thinking activity. Reference is not so much to 'understanding' . . . , but to the creating of new ideas."[1] Diligent individuals are oftentimes innovative thinkers, constantly creating and shaping new ideas.

As valuable as these traits may be to an employer, it is also important to realize their worth to employees. They, too, are recompensed, as Solomon notes in 12:11:

> He who tills his land will have plenty of bread,
> But he who pursues vain things lacks sense.

Though this is not a blanket, absolute promise, the principle Solomon gives here does generally hold true. Those who work diligently in whatever "field" they find themselves will typically reap an adequate harvest to provide for their needs.

A few thoughts later, in verse 24, Solomon implies that the diligent will also be promoted above those who are like the sluggard.

> The hand of the diligent will rule,
> But the slack hand will be put to forced labor.

And, finally, we're told that diligence brings with it a feast of inner satisfaction.

---

1. R. Laird Harris, Gleason L. Archer, Jr., and Bruce K. Waltke, eds., *Theological Wordbook of the Old Testament* (Chicago, Ill.: Moody Press, 1980), vol. 1, p. 330.

The soul of the sluggard craves and gets nothing,
But the soul of the diligent is made fat. . . .
Desire realized is sweet to the soul. (13:4, 19a)

Every disciplined and determined worker relishes the satisfying taste of accomplishment. The natural high that comes from meeting a deadline and finishing a project motivates and lightens our hearts, rather than weighing us down with guilt and regret.

Well, Ms. Diligent, I think we've seen enough to know that you're just the person we've been looking for to oversee some of our operations. When can you start?

The Thoughtful

Actually, we have two kinds of thoughtful workers to consider from Proverbs. Let's start with what makes a *thoughtful boss*.

1. *She is genuinely concerned about the lives of her employees.*

A righteous man has regard for the life of his
   beast,
But the compassion of the wicked is cruel. (12:10)

At first glance, this proverb may seem to have little to do with an employer, but think about it. How many bosses have you known who treated their employees as if they were lowly beasts of burden whose only worth was measured by the load they could carry? More than a few, I suspect. A righteous person, a thoughtful employer, however, shows a genuine concern and compassion for the employee. This same principle is reaffirmed a little later in 27:23.

Know well the condition of your flocks,
And pay attention to your herds.

Isn't it interesting that after years of distancing themselves from their employees, management in corporate America has finally recognized the value of this "thoughtful employer" principle? Companies have been revolutionized by it. Business experts have written books and given seminars to teach this newfound secret of effective management. Only it's not new—this same principle has been patiently waiting to be rediscovered for nearly three thousand years!

2. *He has understanding and insight.*

Like a roaring lion and a rushing bear
Is a wicked ruler over a poor people.

> A leader who is a great oppressor lacks
> understanding. (28:15–16a)

This word picture reproachfully compares the cruel, belligerent tyrant to the most dangerous animals known. Turn it around, though, and we'll find that its opposite is also true: A good leader who resists trampling others with his power has understanding. People don't fear such a boss. They don't run and hide every time he passes, dreading a malicious attack. Instead, they enjoy his presence and instinctively follow his lead.

In the hands of a thoughtful employer, work becomes a place of ministry, an opportunity to build into the lives of others. And the benefit? Those who work *for* you will begin to work *with* you.

The second worker to consider in this category is the *thoughtful employee.*

> He who tends the fig tree will eat its fruit;
> And he who cares for his master will be honored.
> (27:18)

Every thoughtful employee possesses at least two essential traits. (1) He is committed to his job—"tends the fig tree"; and (2) she is loyal to her employer—"cares for his master." Practice these qualities, Solomon says, and the job will yield enjoyable fruit and honor will come your way.

Mr. Thoughtful Leader and Mrs. Thoughtful Worker, your records are impeccable, and it would be a tremendous asset to hire you both. When can you start?

The Skillful

> Do you see a man skilled in his work?
> He will stand before kings;
> He will not stand before obscure men. (22:29)

Think about your own job for a moment. If someone had looked over your shoulder last week, would that individual have witnessed someone who is skilled in his or her work? Are you efficient? Do you possess the technical expertise to carry out your job with competence? Perhaps you need to brush up on new technology, take a refresher course, read a book, or maybe just put more effort into what you do, whether it's being a homemaker, draftsman, plumber, printer, secretary, mechanic, or waitress.

The world desperately needs to see Christians who are skilled in their vocations. That one quality alone will open doors for us to receive respect and a good reputation among non-Christians—doors that might never be opened as wide in any other way. What an impact that would have on the world! It gives a broader meaning to Jesus' words: "Let your light shine before men in such a way that they may see your good [skilled] works, and glorify your Father who is in heaven" (Matt. 5:16).

When can you start?

 Living Insights

Many of us have felt like George Bailey, the main character in the film classic *It's a Wonderful Life*.[2] George has grand visions for his life that always somehow get thwarted, leaving him feeling chained to a very ordinary existence in his little hometown of Bedford Falls.

Finally, in exasperation over a calamity that threatens to close his business and ruin his reputation, George wishes he'd never been born. His wish is granted, and through a frightening barrage of discoveries, he sees how significant his "ordinary" life has actually been. George's diligent, thoughtful, and skillful work at his humble savings and loan impacted many lives and changed the course of the entire town for good.

Like George, many Christians tend to label their lives and activities as important or ordinary, spiritual or secular. Pastoring a church, for example, is important work. Being an electrician isn't. Mission work is spiritual. Stocking food in a grocery store is secular.

But do the Scriptures really teach this kind of categorizing? In their outstanding book *Your Work Matters to God*, authors Doug Sherman and William Hendricks counter this false division.

> There is no distinction between the secular and the sacred. At any moment, no matter what we are doing, we are relating to God either properly or improperly. Thus we need to distinguish, not between secular and sacred, but between sin and righteousness.

2. This Living Insight has been adapted from the study guide *Questions Christians Ask*, coauthored by Lee Hough, from the Bible-teaching ministry of Charles R. Swindoll (Fullerton, Calif.: Insight for Living, 1989), pp. 57–58.

In other words, you can go to church and pray (a "sacred" category) and yet still be in sin. You may recite a creed or partake of the elements yet retain hateful thoughts toward someone who has wronged you. Or sit there and dream about your ambitions, and how fulfilling them will give you esteem, power, or money. . . .

On the other hand, you can go to work in an office where the atmosphere is very "secular"—the conversation is littered with profanity, the jokes are off-color, the work is often slipshod, the politics are wearisome. And yet, like Daniel or Joseph in the Old Testament, you can keep your own conversation pure and your behavior above reproach. You can do your work with integrity, even if others do not. You can honor and obey God in a very worldly environment.

In short, God's interest is not simply that we do holy activities but that we become holy people. Not pious. Not sanctimonious. Not other-worldly. But pure, healthy, Christlike.[3]

Does this biblical perspective challenge or affirm the way you view your work? In what ways?

_____

_____

_____

_____

_____

_____

Like George Bailey, your life and your work make a difference . . . in ways you may never know.

3. Doug Sherman and William Hendricks, *Your Work Matters to God* (Colorado Springs, Colo.: NavPress, 1987), pp. 54–55.

Living Insights

I don't think I'll ever forget it. It was windy, bitter cold, and there I was digging in a ditch in downtown Dallas. People in immaculate three-piece power suits and designer dresses swirled past me like I was just a part of the shrubbery we were putting in. The only people who did seem to notice me were the con men and the derelicts. Everywhere I looked—the limousines, the towers of polished granite, the designer boutiques, the leather briefcases— everything flaunted success and purpose at a time when I felt utterly a failure, without any purpose.

It was a period of deep testing in my life. In an earlier time, in a more comfortable setting, I had vigorously defended the truth that we can glorify God with our work no matter how mundane or insignificant the world may deem it. But now my wife was pregnant, we were living out of a suitcase from one friend's house to the next, and I barely made enough pushing that dirt around to even buy groceries.

Suddenly all that talk about "whatever you do, do your work heartily as for the Lord" hung in the balance. Mere words or solid truth to sustain me in my worst nightmare? Now was my chance to find out. Dig holes with diligence? Be thoughtful knee-deep in dirt on a crowded sidewalk? Weld with skill an iron grating beneath the ground that no one would ever see?

Maybe you're struggling as I was in your job right now. Perhaps it's not glamorous. It may even be monotonous or seemingly insignificant in comparison to what you see others doing around you. Will you still do your work heartily as for the Lord?

Brainstorm some practical ways you can exhibit each of the three qualities studied in the lesson.

Diligence

_____

_____

_____

_____

_____

_____

Thoughtfulness

_____

_____

_____

_____

_____

_____

_____

_____

Skillfulness

_____

_____

_____

_____

_____

_____

_____

_____

Chapter 11

YOU AND YOUR COUNSELING

(PART ONE)

Selected Proverbs

Would you call yourself a counselor? Most of us wouldn't; not unless we have earned an advanced degree in psychology and are licensed to practice. Nowadays even many pastors defer counseling to those considered to be "trained professionals."

Granted, in certain cases it is best to rely on professionals skilled at untying particular mental or emotional knots. But is it necessary all the time? Are we being too quick to disqualify ourselves as capable counselors for many of life's everyday tangles?

The apostle Paul thought so. Listen to his words from Romans 15.

> As far as I am concerned about you, my brothers,
> I am convinced that you especially are abounding
> in the highest goodness, richly supplied with perfect
> knowledge and competent to counsel one another.
> (Rom. 15:14 WILLIAMS)

The Apostle wasn't addressing a convention of psychotherapists here; he was speaking to all the Christians in Rome, many of whom were slaves. So what did he mean by *counsel?* Let's turn to the Old Testament to find out.

What Is Meant by "Counseling" in the Old Testament?

Throughout the Law and the Prophets, the writers used basically four Hebrew words to signify *counsel, counseling,* and *counselor.*

1. *Dabar* (pronounced "dah-baar"). This word is occasionally translated *counsel* (see Num. 31:16). Most often, however, it indicates ordinary, everyday talking, as in Deuteronomy 11:18–19.

> "You shall therefore impress these words of mine
> on your heart and on your soul; and you shall bind
> them as a sign on your hand, and they shall be as
> frontals on your forehead. And you shall teach them
> to your sons, *talking* of them when you sit in your

house and when you walk along the road and when
you lie down and when you rise up." (emphasis added)

Parents needn't wait for trained professionals in the church to
expose their children to biblical truth. They are to *dabar* their
children in the normal over-the-dinner-table, around-the-home,
and out-in-the-neighborhood conversations. Much of what passes
for normal exchanges among family members and friends is actually
a low-key form of counseling.

2. *Sod* ("sohd"). A second term with a slightly different shade
of meaning is found in the first half of Proverbs 15:22.

> Without *consultation*, plans are frustrated,
> But with many counselors they succeed.
> (emphasis added)

"Consultation," translated *sod*, means "being brought close together for the purpose of secret communication and counsel."[1] It
differs from *dabar* in that an ingredient of confidentiality has been
added. When someone asks to speak to you privately about a matter,
that's *sod*.

In Psalm 64:2, *sod* is linked with the word *rigshah*, whose root
is *ragash*, meaning to "be in tumult or commotion."[2] This reminds
us that sometimes counseling can be a tumultuous, stormy experience, especially if the person being counseled is resistant to the
truth and sin is deeply entrenched in the person's life. Resistance
doesn't necessarily mean that you've made a mistake. Rather, it may
be a signal that you as the counselor are on the right track in helping the person confront his or her sin.

3. *Chabal* ("cha-bahl"). Another term for *counsel* is used in 1:5:

> A wise man will hear and increase in learning,
> And a man of understanding will acquire wise
> counsel.

The word Solomon uses for "counsel" comes from the root term
chabal, meaning "to bind or to pledge." Originally, this word was

---

1. C. F. Keil and F. Delitzsch, *Commentary on the Old Testament* (reprint; Grand Rapids,
Mich.: William B. Eerdmans Publishing Co., 1978), vol. 6, p. 328.

2. Francis Brown, S. R. Driver, and Charles A. Briggs, *The New Brown-Driver-Briggs-Gesenius
Hebrew and English Lexicon* (Peabody, Mass.: Hendrickson Publishers, 1979), p. 121.

used of "rope-pulling, i.e. steering, directing a ship."[3] It's the idea of giving specific direction to someone, pulling that person along with a binding agreement or project to correct his or her course.

4. *Yaats* ("yah-ahtz"). The next term, found in 12:20, is used more widely than any other.

> Deceit is in the heart of those who devise evil,
> But counselors of peace have joy.

A popular counseling technique today defines the counselor's role as one of neutral observation, someone who simply listens and reflects what the other person is saying—without making any judgments or offering any advice. Certainly, counselors need to listen and gather information at the beginning. But then to sit there, knowing the help this other person needs but not telling him or her is completely foreign to the biblical view of counseling. To give wise *yaats* means sharing direct, objective information.

The New Testament equivalent is *noutheteō,* "admonish" (Rom. 15:14), which means "to put into the mind." That's what counseling involves—imparting truth to the minds of troubled and confused individuals.

Combining the meanings of all four words into one definition, we might say this:

> *Counseling involves communicating with someone for the purpose of clarifying, instructing, or changing areas of his or her life that need attention.*

Occasionally, this is done in a formal setting with a professional. More often, however, it occurs informally in the casual exchanges of everyday living: friends clarifying issues for friends; parents instructing children; one person impacting another by something he says or she does, sometimes without even knowing it.

Does Counseling Yield Specific Benefits?

For years, the Christian community has been leery of counseling. We have shunned this practice out of fear and ignorance. Solomon, however, understood its positive benefits and mentions at least four in Proverbs.

3. William Gesenius, *A Hebrew and English Lexicon of the Old Testament,* trans. Edward Robinson, ed. Francis Brown, S. R. Driver, Charles A. Briggs (Oxford, England: Clarendon Press, n.d.), p. 287.

First, *to help heal and relieve anxiety.*

> There is one who speaks rashly like the thrusts of
>   a sword,
> But the tongue of the wise brings healing. . . .
> Anxiety in the heart of a man weighs it down,
> But a good word makes it glad. (12:18, 25)

No one can escape the bumps and bruises that come from living in a fallen world. But the tongue of the wise can act like a balm, therapeutic and soothing. It strengthens our inner spirits to fight the infection of anxiety.

Second, *to help us find maximum fulfillment in life.*

> Where there is no guidance, the people fall,
> But in abundance of counselors there is victory.
> (11:14)

Everyone's perspective is limited. Wise counsel from a variety of viewpoints provides a fuller, more accurate picture of the options available in our lives. The wisdom and insight of good friends can blow away the fog of self-doubt, opening our eyes to possibilities God has in store for us (see Eph. 3:20). They can show us the way to make our hopes come true and our lives fulfilled.

> Hope deferred makes the heart sick,
> But desire fulfilled is a tree of life. (Prov. 13:12)

Third, *to help us plan correctly.*

> Without consultation, plans are frustrated,
> But with many counselors they succeed. . . .
> Prepare plans by consultation,
> And make war by wise guidance. (15:22; 20:18)

Are you seeking God's will about something important? A career move? A marriage choice? A business decision? Is there someone in your life who, for some unknown reason, has declared war on you? Someone you need to proceed with caution around? You aren't the first person to struggle through such issues, so be wise! Draw from the vast pool of counselors whose experience can guide you in what paths to take . . . and which to avoid.

Fourth, *to help us become wise, to see life through the lens of God's divine viewpoint.*

Through presumption comes nothing but strife,
But with those who receive counsel is wisdom. . . .
Listen to counsel and accept discipline,
That you may be wise the rest of your days.
(13:10; 19:20)

How skewed our world's perspective is when it applauds as "confident" and "sure of themselves" those who presume to know what's best for them—apart from God's input. Their lives are scarred and circumvented by their own foolish thinking and choices; frustration and bitterness batter their spirits.

But when we are humble, open to the truth of our need and responsive toward change, then wisdom and its rewards define our days. Seeking and being receptive to counsel is the thing to commend—save ridicule for presumption.

Which Ingredients Make Some Counselors More Effective Than Others?

Let's benefit from more of Solomon's wisdom by examining eight traits of an effective counselor from the book of Proverbs. We'll cover the first five in the remainder of this chapter and the final three in the next.

Purity of Life

Young and old, Christians needing wisdom should seek out those who are skilled in godly living.

But the path of the righteous is like the light of
dawn,
That shines brighter and brighter until the full day.
The way of the wicked is like darkness;
They do not know over what they stumble.
(4:18–19)

People respect a pure life because it gives off a light that attracts those who are lost and confused. Walk in the Spirit and you won't have to hang a shingle; the weary and heavy-laden will beat a path to your door.

Confidentiality

We touched on this same issue earlier, remember, in the chapter dealing with the wrong uses of the tongue.

He who goes about as a talebearer reveals secrets,
But he who is trustworthy conceals a matter. . . .
Argue your case with your neighbor,
And do not reveal the secret of another.
(11:13; 25:9)

One of the most basic requirements of a good counselor is a closed mouth. Confidentiality breeds security and trust, essentials that foster freedom in communicating. If you're a name-dropper, if you can't bury forever information that is shocking or scandalous, then you're not qualified to have others share their personal shortcomings and hurts with you. An effective counselor respects the power of information and wields it with extreme discretion.

Timing and Tact

A third quality of a good counselor is found in 15:23 and 28.

A man has joy in an apt answer,
And how delightful is a timely word! . . .
The heart of the righteous ponders how to answer,
But the mouth of the wicked pours out evil things.

The timing of a word is often as important as the words themselves. Competent counselors are patient, slow to speak, and quick to listen. They wait for the appropriate moment to give a precise word of counsel instead of insensitively dumping everything they know on someone the first moment there's a pause.

In addition to knowing when to speak, worthy counselors also ponder how to say things. They understand the power of words and carefully craft each question and response.

Keen Attention and Concentration

He who gives an answer before he hears,
It is folly and shame to him. (18:13)

When was the last time you were in a conversation with someone who kept interrupting you? You've met the kind. They can hardly wait—sometimes *don't* wait—for you to finish talking so they can begin pontificating. They're really not interested in your thoughts or feelings, only in espousing their own.

A quality counselor, however, is a good listener. He looks you in the eye, not over the shoulder or around the room. She concentrates, blocking out all other distractions so she can hear what's being said, as well as what's not being said. They probe, ask clarifying questions, seek to understand so they can offer true empathy and accurate advice.

Objectivity and Discernment

An effective counselor also avoids the trap of making snap judgments based on first impressions.

> The first to plead his case seems just,
> Until another comes and examines him. (v. 17)

Objectivity waits to hear both sides of the story. It allows discernment to search below the surface to find the root issues. "Pretty words may hide a wicked heart," Solomon wrote, "just as a pretty glaze covers a common clay pot" (26:23 LB). Perceptive counselors are not easily sidetracked. They know how to get past the glaze of our self-protection to touch the common clay of our painful needs or our sinful humanity.

As you can tell by now, it takes more than just technical skill to be an effective counselor. The qualities we've examined are ones we can all possess without having to attend graduate school. Before we consider the remaining traits in the next chapter, let's pause to reflect on the truths covered so far.

 Living Insights

Some people think that counseling removes personal responsibility by blaming our past for our present behavior. Or it's there simply to make us happy—cheerful adulterers, contented frauds, or merry alcoholics. But this has nothing to do with the biblical concept of counseling.

What do you think should be the overarching benefit or goal of Christian counseling? Of your counsel to others? In one or two words, sum up what you find in each of the following passages, then write down a composite definition from what you learned from them.

Romans 12:1–2 _____

Ephesians 4:20–24; 5:1–2 _____

Philippians 1:9–10 _____

Colossians 1:28 _____

Hebrews 6:1a _____

1 Peter 1:14–16 _____

Composite Definition

_____
_____
_____
_____

Living Insights

Take a moment to measure your own effectiveness as a counselor using the five traits from our study in Proverbs. (One is the weakest on this scale.)

Purity of Life

1   2   3   4   5   6   7   8   9   10

Confidentiality

1   2   3   4   5   6   7   8   9   10

Timing and Tact

1   2   3   4   5   6   7   8   9   10

Keen Attention and Concentration (A Good Listener)

1   2   3   4   5   6   7   8   9   10

Objectivity and Discernment

1   2   3   4   5   6   7   8   9   10

Using the same scale, what number would you choose to signify the overall effectiveness of your counseling? _____

Chapter 12

YOU AND YOUR COUNSELING
(PART TWO)
Selected Proverbs

J ust as our physical bodies need water, so our invisible inner souls need understanding. We thirst for it in our spirits. It is one of our deepest longings, one that we constantly seek to quench. And each time someone gives us a drink from its cup, our hearts are refreshed.

Effective counselors are a well of understanding to those who come to them. With Solomon's help, let's explore this quality and two others in our list of traits of an effective counselor.

More Qualities That Make Us Effective Counselors

Understanding

> As in water face reflects face,
> So the heart of man reflects man. (Prov. 27:19)

Commentators Keil and Delitzsch draw out the meaning of this verse for us:

> The thought is beautiful: as in the water-mirror each one beholds his own face . . . , so out of the heart of another each sees his own heart, *i.e.* he finds in another the dispositions and feelings of his own heart . . . the face finds in water its reflection, and the heart of a man finds in man its echo; . . . it is a fortunate thing that their heart is capable of the same sympathetic feelings, so that one can pour into the heart of another that which fills and moves his own heart, and can there find . . . a re-echo.[1]

How exactly can we communicate this gift of understanding? The first of two significant attitudes that convey it is *acceptance*.

1. C. F. Keil and F. Delitzsch, *Commentary on the Old Testament* (reprint; Grand Rapids, Mich.: William B. Eerdmans Publishing Co., 1978), vol. 6, pp. 214–15.

Now, this doesn't necessarily mean approving of what someone has done or said or plans to do. It simply means loving the person; showing the same kind of unconditional love God pours out on us all, sinner and saint alike.

Unfortunately, many of us exude rejection more than acceptance. We constantly pass judgment on others with harsh words like, "You're just a troublemaker," or, "He got what he deserved," or, "She'll never learn. Helping her is just a waste of time." Rejection kills the spirit of the one giving it as well as the one receiving it. We should learn, instead, to accept, to affirm the God-given value instilled in every human being no matter who they are or what they've done.

A second way to communicate understanding is through a *willingness to get involved*. The uninvolved look around the room, say "hello" to passersby, or continue doing piddly work while you talk. But you can usually tell a person of understanding simply by reading his or her eyes, posture, and words. They invite you in, encourage you to unburden yourself, reaffirm that they care and want to help.

Honesty

The seventh crucial characteristic is found in 24:23–26.

> These also are sayings of the wise.
> To show partiality in judgment is not good.
> He who says to the wicked, "You are righteous,"
> Peoples will curse him, nations will abhor him;
> But to those who rebuke the wicked will be delight,
> And a good blessing will come upon them.
> He kisses the lips
> Who gives a right answer.

This particular passage reminded Chuck of a painfully heated counseling session he had once with a young couple. When it was over, the wife wiped the tears from her eyes and said, "Thank you for telling us the truth, for being honest. I hated you for it at the time . . . but I would have hated you more if you'd have fudged. We needed to hear the truth."

In the final analysis, people who really want help will appreciate your telling them the truth. Solomon affirmed this when he wrote,

> He who rebukes a man will afterward find more favor
> Than he who flatters with the tongue. (28:23)

97

Speak the truth. Don't gloss over wrong (25:26). But remember, as we noted in the last chapter, to pay special attention to the timing and tact of your words (see 15:4). The truth can hurt. And we can either wield it carelessly as a blunt instrument to wound, or we can use it skillfully as a surgeon's scalpel to heal.

Genuine Interest and Love

Last, each time we apply the previous seven traits to our counseling, the fragrance of genuine interest and love will linger long in the memory of the one counseled.

> Oil and perfume make the heart glad,
> So a man's counsel is sweet to his friend. (27:9)

Jonathan's counsel was sweet to David during a very bitter time in his life (see 1 Sam. 19–20; 23:15–18). Paul's counsel surely made Timothy's heart glad when he felt weak and afraid (1 Tim. 4:11–16; 2 Tim. 1:1–14). Why? Was it simply because of the truth David and Timothy received? No, it was because that truth was communicated by close friends whom they knew loved them deeply.

Now that we've examined these eight qualities that make a counselor effective, one question still remains.

Is Counseling Always Successful?

Can any counselor, no matter how well he or she exemplifies tact, objectivity, understanding, and the rest, guarantee the outcome of their advice? Absolutely not. Because even at our best, we are still human and make mistakes. A missed clue or wrong conclusion is all that it takes. Then, too, we're not always given enough time to probe for understanding. And in some cases, no amount of counsel will help because the root problem is medical in origin.

But if a counselor could avoid all those problems, would he or she then always be successful? No again, and Proverbs gives us several reasons why.

1. The Counsel Is Ignored

> He is on the path of life who heeds instruction,
> But he who forsakes reproof goes astray. (10:17)

The results of any counseling situation ultimately rest in the hands of the counselees. They may be given the best advice, but if they choose to disregard it, nothing will change.

2. They Only Want to Talk

> A fool does not delight in understanding,
> But only in revealing his own mind. (18:2)

Like the fool, many seek counseling not because they desire insight, direction, or reproof, but because they simply enjoy telling others about their woes. As long as you listen, they'll praise you as a wise and loving counselor. Uncover some of their inadequacies, however, and suddenly you'll find yourself written off as an insensitive brute.

3. They Don't Desire to Change

> A man of great anger shall bear the penalty,
> For if you rescue him, you will only have to do it
> again. (19:19)

Solomon specifically addresses the angry person who finds greater pleasure in venting anger than in curbing it. Desire, the will to change and give up old habits to take on new, must be present before lasting change can occur.

4. Some Cover Up and Defend

> When a wise man has a controversy with a
> foolish man,
> The foolish man either rages or laughs, and there
> is no rest. (29:9)

When the counseling hits too close to home, some counselees will attempt to back you off with angry outbursts punctuated with pounding fists and threatening words. Others may laugh inappropriately, as if you had just told the world's funniest joke. All to make you think your advice is nonsense and they can't possibly take it seriously.

5. Simply No Response

> A slave will not be instructed by words alone;
> For though he understands, there will be no
> response. (29:19)

Commentator Derek Kidner sheds some light on this verse: "This apparently sweeping statement (*cf.* 21) is seen, when balanced by others (*e.g.* 17:2), to refer to the slave mentality, unresponsive, irresponsible."[2] As you may recall from our earlier studies, the mentality of the wise is to embrace reproof. The fool, however, hears and understands wisdom's voice, but does not answer her. Why? Perhaps the will to change is not there. Or maybe this individual wants to snub the person bringing the reproof. The possible reasons are too numerous to list. But, the outcome is always the same—no response, no change.

No counselor can control another person's response to ensure success. What we can do when a counseling situation fails is step back and evaluate, "Was there something I did wrong? Did I overlook something?" If you cannot find anything significant, then rest the case with the Lord. Don't wallow in feelings of guilt or discouragement. God has His own timing for causing people to mature. As Paul said in 1 Corinthians 3, "I planted, Apollos watered, but God was causing the growth" (v. 6).

 Living Insights

As you did in the previous lesson, pause for a little self-evaluation. Circle the number that best represents the strength or weakness of the final three traits in your counseling.

Understanding

1   2   3   4   5   6   7   8   9   10

Honesty

1   2   3   4   5   6   7   8   9   10

Genuine Interest and Love

1   2   3   4   5   6   7   8   9   10

Can you think of a biblical character that best exemplifies each of these traits? How? If not, perhaps you know a godly man or woman who models each of these traits.

Understanding

2. Derek Kidner, *The Proverbs: An Introduction and Commentary* (Downers Grove, Ill.: Inter-Varsity Press, 1964), p. 176.

Honesty

Genuine Interest and Love

 Living Insights

Aside from acceptance and a willingness to get involved, what are some other meaningful ways to communicate understanding? For example, body language, the use of questions—think of things that help you know when you're understood.

_____

_____

_____

◆

Proverbs 29:11 states, "A fool gives full vent to his anger" (NIV). Some people call that being honest. But, as Jay Adams points out in his book *Competent to Counsel,*

> The idea of allowing anger to break out in an un-disciplined manner by saying or doing whatever comes into mind without weighing the consequences, without counting ten, without holding it back and quieting it, without hearing the whole story, is totally wrong. . . . Ventilating sinful feelings is simply unbiblical. The words "full vent" . . . mean literally "to send forth all of one's spirit."[3]

3. Jay E. Adams, *Competent to Counsel* (Phillipsburg, N.J.: Presbyterian and Reformed Publishing Co., 1972), p. 221.

Do you sometimes send forth all of your spirit in the name of honesty? Do the people you counsel come away feeling built up and encouraged or bloodied and humiliated? Give a word picture that best describes how you speak the truth in counseling situations.

_____

_____

_____

_____

_____

◆

"Susan and I have been fighting a lot lately."

"Oh? What's the problem?"

"Money. We can't seem to agree on . . . ."

"Have you ever read Larry Burkett's or Ron Blue's books on finances? I tell ya, you and Susan just need to work through some of their books together, and your problems would be over."

"Really?"

"Yeah, great stuff. Since I started following their advice, me and Vicky never fight over finances. You guys will be the same. You'll do fine. Besides, at least you're not in Wilson's shoes. Talk about problems. He went chapter 11 last week and Charlene left him. Well, listen, I gotta run. Get those books. I'll be praying for you."

Look carefully at this casual moment of counseling between two friends, and note all the ways genuine interest and love was or was not communicated. For every negative example you find, give a positive solution.

Negative Example	Positive Solution
_____	_____
_____	_____
_____	_____
_____	_____

Chapter 13

YOU AND YOUR HEART

Selected Proverbs

Beeeeeeee—
Emergency, Code Blue!—*eeeeeeeeeeeeeee*—*Start chest compression.*
Get the intubation ready. Someone bag first—*eeeeeeeee*—*Begin an epi*
1 milligram IV push—*eeeeeeeee*—*no change; continue compression*—
eeeeeeeeee—Listen for breathing. Time? Four minutes—Let's shock
him, 300 watts—*eeeeeeeee*—paddles ready. Everybody clear!
WHUMP—Rhythm check for pulse—*eeeeeee*—Still nothing. We're
losing him—*eeeeeee*—Another epi. Increase watts to 360—*eeeeeee*
eeeee—Charging . . .

It's hard to imagine that it could be you or me whose heart
stops like this one day. Most of the time we're not even aware of
the fist-sized muscle within our breasts that dutifully beats more
than one hundred thousand times a day. Nor are we conscious of
its powerful contractions that propel oxygen and nutrition through
more than sixty thousand miles of arteries, veins, and capillaries.
Yet when it hurts, we're in serious trouble. When it fails, we die.
And thousands are dying every day because of heart disease.

Even more epidemic, however, is the problem of spiritual heart
disease. You see, within each of us God has implanted another
"heart" we're often not aware of, whose beat reverberates in nearly
a thousand references in Scripture. Proverbs alone pulses with it
more than sixty-five times and in all but three of its chapters. Like
its physical counterpart, this intangible eternal organ is also suscep-
tible to disease. Sin has infected the heart of all Christians, causing

The section in this chapter entitled "What Does the Term *Heart* Mean?" has been adapted
from the study guide *A Ministry Everyone Would Respect*, coauthored by Ken Gire, from the Bible-
teaching ministry of Charles R. Swindoll (Fullerton, Calif.: Insight for Living, 1989), pp. 96–97.

all kinds of carnal coronary conditions. That's why Solomon warns,

> Watch over your heart with all diligence,
> For from it flow the springs of life. (Prov. 4:23)

. . . *All clear!* WHUMP—*eeeeeeeeee* *I'm getting a pulse.*

Blood pressure? Eighty over 50 *C'mon baby, beat!*

He's gonna make it

I've got 100 over 60. He made it!

But will we—spiritually speaking? Just how healthy is your heart? Has sin blocked the flow of your prayers? Is your faith easily winded? Are you experiencing a numbing sensation in your conscience that makes it difficult to discern between good and evil? Many of us have similar symptoms. We're dangerously close to having a cardiac arrest.

Instead of waiting until we need 360 watts of scorching reproof to revive our hearts, why not stay healthy by practicing the type of preventive care Solomon prescribes in Proverbs? Interested? Then let's join him in the operating theater and conduct a thorough examination of the heart laid bare in Proverbs.

What Does the Term *Heart* Mean?

Biblically, the term *heart* represents our whole inner being. This is how the word is used in 1 Samuel 16:7:

> The Lord said to Samuel, "Do not look at his appearance or at the height of his stature, because I have rejected him; for God sees not as man sees, for man looks at the outward appearance, but the Lord looks at the heart."

In Proverbs, the Hebrew word predominantly used for *heart* is *leb*. It "not only includes the motives, feelings, affections, and desires, but also the will, the aims, the principles, the thoughts, and the intellect."[1]

The Greek word for *heart* is *kardia*, from which we form such words as *cardiology*. Gerhard Kittel, in his massive, nine-volume work on New Testament words, describes the term as follows:

> The heart is the centre of the inner life of man and the source or seat of all the forces and functions of soul and spirit. . . . Thus *[kardia]* comes to stand for the whole of the inner being of man in contrast to his external side. . . . The heart is supremely the one centre in man to which God turns, in which the religious life is rooted, which determines moral conduct.[2]

From Proverbs 2:2 to 31:11 Solomon repeatedly mentions the heart and, in doing so, provides us with a detailed picture of its inner workings. Let's look now at the wide variety of heart specimens he has on display.

Are There Various Kinds of Hearts?

Even a cursory glance of Proverbs reveals a broad diversity of hearts. For example:

A scheming heart (6:18a)	A righteous heart (15:28)
A cunning, sensual heart (7:9–10)	A glad heart (15:30)
A wise heart (10:8)	A haughty heart (18:12)
A deceptive heart (12:20)	A heart of rage (19:3)
A hurting heart (14:13)	A pure heart (22:11)
A tranquil heart (14:30)	An envious heart (23:17)

What is it that determines the kind of heart we will have? First of all, our *thoughts*: "For as he thinks within himself, so he is" (23:7a). We are what we think about. Someone once illustrated this beautifully, saying, "Sow a thought, reap an act. Sow an act, reap a habit. Sow a habit, reap your character. Sow your character, reap your destiny." It all begins with the seed thoughts we allow to flourish in our minds.

1. Robert Baker Girdlestone, *Synonyms of the Old Testament*, 2d ed. (1897; reprint, Grand Rapids, Mich.: William B. Eerdmans Publishing Co., n.d.), p. 65.

2. Gerhard Kittel, ed., *Theological Dictionary of the New Testament*, trans. Geoffrey W. Bromiley (Grand Rapids, Mich.: William B. Eerdmans Publishing Co., 1965), vol. 3, pp. 611–12.

A second major influence that molds the heart is our *speech*. "Death and life are in the power of the tongue" (18:21a). The tongue does more than just reveal what's in our hearts, it sparks other thoughts and consumes the thoughts of others around us. James warns, "Behold, how great a forest is set aflame by such a small fire! And the tongue . . . sets on fire the course of our life" (James 3:5b, 6b).

Third, our hearts are shaped by how we spend our *money*. "For where your treasure is, there will your heart be also" (Luke 12:34). What receives the greatest investment of your time and money? Your car, boat, home, hobby? Examine your checkbook. Read the expenditures like they were directions on a map and you'll likely find where your treasure is buried.

How about Specific Actions Prompted by the Heart?

Proverbs also reveals that the heart initiates certain bents or mind-sets. Let's move the stethoscope of our attention around to four different passages and listen carefully for the specific action in each.

First: Spurns Reproof (5:12–13)

And you say, "How I have hated instruction!
And my heart spurned reproof!
And I have not listened to the voice of my teachers,
Nor inclined my ear to my instructors!"

Whoa! Watch your ears. The rebellious son pictured here fairly shouts as he recounts with agonizing self-reproach the many times he's refused wisdom. He has scoffed at his instructors, teachers, whomever wisdom put in his path. How many children have this same heart? How many aged? Solomon tells us in 10:8, "The wise of heart will receive commands." Humbly receive or pridefully reject—which response characterizes your heart?

Second: Bent on Sensuality (6:23–25a; 7:24–25a)

For the commandment is a lamp, and the teaching
is light;
And reproofs for discipline are the way of life,
To keep you from the evil woman,
From the smooth tongue of the adulteress.
Do not desire her beauty *in your heart*. . . .
Now therefore, my sons, listen to me,

And pay attention to the words of my mouth.
Do not let your *heart* turn aside to her ways.
(emphasis added)

Notice that lust springs from a heart desire. And for various reasons, the heart of some individuals pumps nothing but the lurid and immoral into their imaginations. To cleanse the flow of our inner thoughts we must follow Solomon's practical advice. For example, be selective about what we allow our eyes to bring into our hearts (4:25–27); meditate on and obey wisdom's teachings (6:20–22); and don't resuscitate the sensual heart by dwelling on impure thoughts (v. 25a).

Third: Anxiety and Gloom (12:25a; 18:14)

Anxiety in the heart of a man weighs it down. . . .
The spirit of a man can endure his sickness,
But a broken spirit who can bear?

Anxiety anchors our spirits in a dark abyss of gloomy uncertainty and fear. Everything seems negative. Our laughter may take on a hollow ring: "Even in laughter the heart may be in pain, And the end of joy may be grief" (14:13). Only the heart unfettered with anxiety can experience the light buoyancy of joy.

A tranquil heart is life to the body. . . .
A joyful heart makes a cheerful face,
But when the heart is sad, the spirit is broken. . . .
All the days of the afflicted are bad,
But a cheerful heart has a continual feast.
(14:30a; 15:13, 15; see also 17:22)

Fourth: Indiscriminate Sharing (18:2)

A fool does not delight in understanding,
But only in revealing his own mind.

The verse literally says, "in revealing all of his *heart*" (emphasis added). Compare this to the verse in Judges 16, where Samson told Delilah "all that was in his heart" concerning the secret of his strength (v. 17). That indiscretion of indiscriminate sharing cost him his strength, his freedom, his eyes, and, ultimately, his life. Fools speak without thinking, and their careless babbling is their undoing. The wise, however, restrain words for their appropriate timing (see Prov. 12:23). They know when to cease talking and when to be transparent. "Like apples of gold in settings of silver," Solomon wrote, "Is a word spoken in right circumstances" (25:11).

Does God Give Us Any Practical Instruction for the Heart?

Today more than ever, people are concerned with eating right and exercising to maintain healthy hearts. We spend billions in a quest for fitness, all the while virtually ignoring the eternal heart that beats within the invisible realm of our spirit. Is it any wonder, then, why so many suffer from a weakened spiritual heart condition that makes it nearly impossible to fight the good fight, finish the course, or keep the faith (see 2 Tim. 4:7)?

As the personal physician for our true hearts, Solomon has already made one important recommendation that we noted at the beginning of this lesson—"Watch over your heart with all diligence, For from it flow the springs of life" (Prov. 4:23). Let's see what practical insights we can draw from these words to guide us in our pursuit of spiritual health.

Notice, first of all, that the verse opens with a command; not a wish, not a suggestion, but a direct order. Second, the reason we're ordered to guard our hearts carefully is explained in the latter half of the verse, "For from it flow the springs of life." Third, this command is given top priority, "with *all* diligence." We're to focus everything at our disposal to accomplish this objective. And, fourth, we're told that the outcome of our entire life depends on how well we obey this order.

The heart is where the Holy Spirit communicates truth. So guard that. Preserve that. "The springs of life" flow from within the holy ground of the heart, meaning God's direction and conviction. Nothing more sacred belongs to you than this vital organ. Keep watch over it well.

 Living Insights STUDY ONE

When was the last time you had your inner heart checked? Perhaps you're about due for a spiritual stress test to measure its overall health. To do this, we've provided you with several cardiograms to chart your heartbeat under varying conditions.

The first graph is a sample to help you see how it works. The main subject to be tested is finances. Now, we put the heart through its paces in this area by indicating how strong or weak our spiritual pulse is under each of the related categories.

SAMPLE: **Finances**

Give Generously	Give Regularly	Save Wisely	Live within My Means	Content with What I Have

Home

Put Others First	Patient with Spouse	Pray Regularly	Model Christ	Family Devotions

Work

Honest	Good Attitude	Servant to Others	Respect Authority	Work Is Above Standard	Initiate Ideas

Friends

Loyal	Truthful	Give Comfort in Conflict	Forgiving	Open	Encouraging

Enemies

Kind	Pray for Them	Refuse to Gossip	Ready to Forgive

God

Bible Study	Prayer	Worship	Good Samaritan Lifestyle

_____
_____
_____
_____

Once you've finished, write a summary of your findings in the space provided.

Test Results

_____

_____

_____

_____

_____

_____

Living Insights   STUDY TWO

As we mentioned in the lesson, Proverbs pulses with the beat of many different kinds of "hearts." To conduct a more in-depth study of their wide variety and their differences, look up in a concordance all the references to *heart* listed under Proverbs. As you read about each one, use the space provided to make observations, comparisons, or groupings. Also, in light of your test results from the first Living Insight, which heart from this study do you feel is most like your own?

Reference   Observations, Comparisons, and Groupings

_____   _____

_____   _____

_____   _____

_____   _____

_____   _____

_____ _____

_____ _____

_____ _____

_____ _____

_____ _____

_____ _____

_____ _____

_____ _____

_____ _____

_____ _____

_____ _____

_____ _____

_____ _____

_____ _____

_____ _____

The Heart(s) Most Like My Own

_____

_____

_____

_____

_____

Chapter 14

THE WOMAN WHO FEARS THE LORD

Proverbs 31; Selected Proverbs

M any women understandably feel intimidated by the Proverbs
31 woman. You know, she's the one who's up before dawn,
still going long after the sun has set, preparing gourmet meals,
spinning Paris-fashion quality clothing, selling handmade goods—
oh, and buying real estate. In fact, on her land she plants not just
a backyard garden but a full-scale vineyard—no doubt to produce
award-winning wines under the family label (which she has, of
course, designed herself).

Martha Stewart, move over!

It *is* intimidating to be measured against someone like her, isn't
it? But you know what? Maybe our problem is that we *shouldn't* be
measuring ourselves against her. Many commentators believe that
Proverbs 31 isn't presenting an ideal wife so much as the personi-
fication of wisdom—Lady Wisdom, if you will.[1] And this lady offers
to show us the way of strength rather than look down her nose and
watch us wallow in our weaknesses. Professor Allen P. Ross explains.

> Wisdom is personified as a woman because the word
> "wisdom" is a feminine noun and naturally suggests
> it, and because the woman is an excellent example of
> wisdom by virtue of the variety of applications . . .
> at home, in the market, with charity, in business. . . .
>
> The poem certainly presents a pattern for
> women who want to develop a life of wisdom; but
> since it is essentially about wisdom, its lessons are
> for both men and women to develop. The passage
> teaches that the fear of the Lord will inspire people
> to be faithful stewards of the time and talents that
> God has given; that wisdom is productive and ben-
> eficial for others, requiring great industry in life's

---

1. Wisdom is presented as a woman throughout Proverbs; see 1:20–33; 3:13–18; 4:6–9; 7:4;
8:1–21; 9:1–12.

endeavors; that wisdom is best taught and lived in the home—indeed, the success of the home demands wisdom—and that wisdom is balanced living, giving attention to domestic responsibilities as well as business enterprises and charitable service.[2]

In addition, Proverbs 31—though providing us with a rich portrait of wisdom framed in a woman's world—is not the only place in Proverbs where women can learn to be wise. The whole book is good for that! To narrow things down, however, let's begin by looking at a few of wisdom's results in Proverbs 31 and then go beyond that to the rest of Proverbs to explore five characteristics of a woman who fears the Lord.

Results of Living Wisely

> An excellent wife, who can find?
> For her worth is far above jewels. (Prov. 31:10)

The New International Version calls this woman "a wife of noble character." She is a woman of "excellence"—of moral strength and practical capability—and is a rare and invaluable find. To be such a woman doesn't require special talents or gleaming résumés. It means being wise and godly—caring, kind, thinking, hardworking, sensitive, aware, imaginative.

What is the outcome of being a woman like this, and particularly a wife like this? First, *she will have her husband's trust:*

> The heart of her husband trusts in her. (v. 11a)

Because she so ably runs her household, her husband has confidence in her. He feels safe and secure—has a sense of well-being—because he believes in his wife. Her character and competence provide a safe haven for his heart.

Second, *she will benefit her husband:*

> And he will have no lack of gain. (v. 11b)

The NIV says that the excellent wife's husband "lacks nothing of value." Interestingly, the Hebrew word for *gain* as well as *value—shalal—*"usually means 'plunder'; the point may be that the gain

---

2. Allen P. Ross, "Proverbs," in *The Expositor's Bible Commentary*, gen. ed. Frank E. Gaebelein (Grand Rapids, Mich.: Zondervan Publishing House, 1991), vol. 5, p. 1130.

will be as rich and bountiful as the spoils of war."[3] Clearly, this woman enriches the life of her husband.

Third, *she will affirm her husband:*

> She does him good and not evil All the days of her
> life. (v. 12)

Commentator Robert Alden tells us that "this woman is dedicated to her husband. All she says and does is meant to support, build up, encourage, and affirm him."[4] Unselfishly and steadfastly, she loves him with a true love, always seeking his highest good.

Last, *she will impress her family:*

> Her children rise up and bless her; Her husband also,
> and he praises her, saying: "Many daughters have
> done nobly, But you excel them all." (vv. 28–29)

The family of an excellent woman, reaping the benefits of her wisdom and kindness and care, not only recognizes her character and work but also responds with grateful praise. Many women go unnoticed and unsung, which makes this family's delight and praise a high reward indeed.

The secret of being an excellent woman is the same as the secret of being wise—living out one's fear (reverential awe) of the Lord:

> Charm is deceitful and beauty is vain,
> But a woman who fears the Lord, she shall be
> praised. (v. 30)

What's involved in being a woman who fears the Lord—a woman of wisdom? Let's turn to the rest of Proverbs and uncover five defining characteristics.

What Characterizes a Woman Who Fears the Lord?

Just as a woman who wants to be excellent doesn't need any special talents or qualifying achievements, so a woman seeking wisdom doesn't need any secret codes or magic keys. Wisdom calls and understanding lifts up her voice (8:1), inviting us into her home to join in the banquet she has prepared (9:1–5). Wisdom is available to all who are eager for her company (see James 1:5–6).

3. Ross, "Proverbs," p. 1130.

4. Robert L. Alden, *Proverbs: A Commentary on an Ancient Book of Timeless Advice* (Grand Rapids, Mich.: Baker Book House, 1983), p. 220.

What can we learn at Lady Wisdom's table? At least five qualities that characterize a woman who fears the Lord.

A Hatred of Evil

Lady Wisdom names this first characteristic in Proverbs 8:13:

> "The fear of the Lord is to hate evil;
> Pride and arrogance and the evil way,
> And the perverted mouth, I hate."

Evil opposes and assaults all that is good, all that is life-giving, all that is God's way. It runs counter to the way things ought to be, as Cornelius Plantinga Jr. explains.

> The webbing together of God, humans, and all creation in justice, fulfillment, and delight is what the Hebrew prophets call *shalom*. We call it peace, but it means far more than mere peace of mind or a cease-fire between enemies. In the Bible, shalom means *universal flourishing, wholeness, and delight*—a rich state of affairs in which natural needs are satisfied and natural gifts fruitfully employed, a state of affairs that inspires joyful wonder as its Creator and Savior opens doors and welcomes the creatures in whom he delights. Shalom, in other words, is the way things ought to be. . . .
>
> The story of the fall tells us that sin corrupts: it puts asunder what God had joined together and joins together what God had put asunder. Like some devastating twister, corruption both explodes and implodes creation, pushing it back toward the "formless void" from which it came. . . .
>
> In sum, shalom is God's design for creation and redemption; sin is blamable human vandalism of these great realities and therefore an affront to their architect and builder.[5]

Evil is anti-God, which means it is anti-love, anti-trust, anti-kindness, anti-peace, anti-joy. As wisdom becomes our companion,

5. Cornelius Plantinga Jr., *Not the Way It's Supposed to Be: A Breviary of Sin* (Grand Rapids, Mich.: William B. Eerdmans Publishing Co., 1995), pp. 10, 30, 27, 16.

we will develop an increased sensitivity toward evil and the pride, arrogance, and perversion it flings in God's face. We will hate what is evil and cling to what is good (see Amos 5:15; Rom. 12:9), for as Solomon reminds us:

> [She] who is steadfast in righteousness will attain
> to life,
> And [she] who pursues evil will bring about [her]
> own death. (Prov. 11:19)

Restrained Lips and a Controlled Tongue

The next trait Lady Wisdom instills is discreet speech:

> Wise [women] store up knowledge,
> But with the mouth of the foolish, ruin is at hand.
> (10:14)

> When there are many words, transgression is
> unavoidable,
> But [she] who restrains [her] lips is wise. (v. 19)

> The heart of the righteous ponders how to answer,
> But the mouth of the wicked pours out evil things.
> (15:28)

> [She] who guards [her] mouth and [her] tongue,
> Guards [her] soul from troubles. (21:23)

Wisdom teaches us to avoid blurting out the first thing that comes to mind. It teaches us to silently "store up knowledge" for the right occasion,[6] take time to think before speaking, and carefully weigh how to say something so it is the least hurtful and the most beneficial. Indiscriminate and insensitive speech can cause a lot of harm, but when wisdom guides us to say the right thing at the right time, much good can result:

> There is one who speaks rashly like the thrusts of a
> sword,
> But the tongue of the wise brings healing.
> (12:18; see also 15:23; 16:24; 25:11)

---

6. Derek Kidner, *Proverbs: An Introduction and Commentary*, Tyndale Old Testament Commentaries series (Downers Grove, Ill.: InterVarsity Press, 1964), p. 87.

Emotional Stability

Because wisdom protects us from hurt and leads us toward peace and security, we will become more emotionally stable as we grow wiser. Proverbs 14:26 reminds us of where wisdom is rooted—the reverence of God.

> In the fear of the Lord there is strong confidence,
> And his children will have refuge.

When we revere and obey the Lord, we put our confidence in Him and in His Spirit who is at work within us. He will guide us in ways of honor (3:35); prudence, knowledge, and discretion (8:12); life (13:14; 14:27); safety (14:3); goodness (19:8); strength (24:5); confident hope (24:14; 31:25b); peace (29:8); self-control (29:11); and dignity (31:25a). What more could calm our spirits than ways like these?

In contrast, the adulterous woman—the woman who walks in rebellion against God's ways—

> does not ponder the path of life;
> Her ways are unstable, she does not know it. (5:6)

This woman isn't even aware of how shaky her life's foundation is. Her road is crooked, filled with perilous turns and drop-offs she doesn't think about. The woman who loves and obeys the Lord, however, is led

> in the ways of wisdom;
> I have led you in upright paths.
> When you walk, your steps will not be impeded;
> And if you run, you will not stumble. . . .
> The path of life leads upward for the wise,
> That [she] may keep away from Sheol below.
> (4:11–12; 15:24)

A Listening Ear, a Teachable Spirit

A fourth trait Lady Wisdom bestows is a listening, open spirit.

> [She] whose ear listens to the life-giving reproof
> Will dwell among the wise.
> [She] who neglects discipline despises [herself],
> But [she] who listens to reproof acquires
>   understanding.

The fear of the Lord is the instruction for
    wisdom,
And before honor comes humility.
(15:31–33; see also 18:15)

Do you know what underlies these thoughts? Humility of heart. Only a humble person is teachable. Only a humble person will see that another's needs are just as important as her own. Only a humble person will close her mouth to listen to someone else's words. As Kidner observes, "Those who know most know best how little they know."[7]

A Heart Free of Envy

The last gift of Lady Wisdom's that we'll look at is a heart that's free and clear of envy.

Do not let your heart envy sinners,
But live in the fear of the Lord always.
Surely there is a future,
And your hope will not be cut off. (23:17–18)

Do not be envious of evil men,
Nor desire to be with them;
For their minds devise violence,
And their lips talk of trouble. (24:1–2)

When people cheat on taxes and save a bundle while we're honest and wind up paying; when they get to the top of their field at any cost while we're the nice guys who always seem to finish last; when others have love affairs while we remain celibate (and lonely) until marriage; when those who don't give a thought to God get expensive homes with luxurious furnishings while we're tithing, supporting charities, and barely making ends meet, it's easy to start coveting.

Who of us hasn't been tempted to throw in the towel on Christianity and just go for what we want when we want it with whomever we want? How Satan plays on our shortsightedness! Kidner says that this kind of envy springs "from an undue preoccupation with oneself and with the present. The remedy is to look up"—to the Lord (23:17b)—"and look ahead"—to our eternal future and hope (v. 18a).[8]

7. Kidner, *Proverbs*, p. 129.

8. Kidner, *Proverbs*, p. 152.

There's another kind of envy, however, that goes beyond wanting the easy-looking lifestyle of those who don't worry about God. Sometimes we resent others for their possessions, or their talents and position, or even the blessings God has given them. Cain envied Abel's acceptance by God and killed him for it. Saul envied the praise David received for slaying Goliath and tried for years to kill him. Haman envied Mordecai's attention from the king and sought to kill him. The violence that envy can generate distinguishes it from covetousness, as Plantinga reveals.

> To covet is to want somebody else's good so strongly . . . that one is tempted to steal it. To envy is to resent somebody else's good so much that one is tempted to destroy it. The coveter has empty hands and wants to fill them with somebody else's goods. The envier has empty hands and therefore wants to empty the hands of the envied. Envy, moreover, carries overtones of personal resentment: an envier resents not only somebody else's blessing but also the one who has been blessed. . . .
>
> When he acts on his resentment, the envier typically assumes the role of a vandal. He's out to mar, to deface, to despoil, to destroy. His target may be a reputation, a dream, a piece of property, a peaceful state of mind, or even a human life. . . .
>
> The envious vandal cannot let beauty, riches, or wholeness be. At his worst, he resents anything that is really healthy or flourishing. He'd veto heaven itself if he could. Confronted by beauty or blessing, what an envier wants to do is to raise Cain. The envier is a child of the evil one: if he cannot have heaven, he can at least raise hell in the lives of others.[9]

Envy is a path that leads to death, a malignancy that eats away the soul. It contains the cancers of pride, anger, and resentment. It fills us with the delusion that we're our own gods and that things must always go the way we want. Radical repentance is needed to excise envy; we must humble ourselves before the one true God and gratefully accept what He deems appropriate to give us. Only

9. Plantinga, *Not the Way It's Supposed to Be*, pp. 162, 164.

when we dethrone ourselves and enthrone Him in His proper place will we know contentment. As Solomon urges:

> Listen, my [daughter], and be wise,
> And direct your heart in the way. (23:19)

Concluding Thought

One other gift that Lady Wisdom bestows is balance. Being wise enables us to avoid fanatical extremes and actually become easier to live with. As Solomon pictured:

> By wisdom a house is built,
> And by understanding it is established;
> And by knowledge the rooms are filled
> With all precious and pleasant riches. (24:3–4)

May wisdom's precious and pleasant riches begin to fill your house as a result of your study in Proverbs!

 Living Insights _____ STUDY ONE

What characteristic of a woman who fears the Lord are you excelling in? How have you grown in this area?

_____

_____

_____

What trait do you need to grow in? How has your weakness in this area manifested itself?

_____

_____

_____

What changes do you need to make in order to foster your growth?

_____

_____

What other characteristics can you think of, perhaps in women you know, that adorn the life of a wise and godly woman?

_____

_____

_____

 Living Insights

In her tribute to humorist Erma Bombeck at her memorial service, Norma Born read a poem titled "The Measure of a Woman" that seems a fitting close to our study. Read it slowly, and let it work its way into your heart.

> Not—"How did she die?" But—"How did she live?"
> Not—"What did she gain?" But—"What did
>   she give?"
> These are the units to measure the worth
> Of a woman as a woman, regardless of birth.
>
> Not—"What was her station?" But—"Had she
>   a heart?"
> And—"How did she play her God-given part?"
> Was she ever ready with a word of good cheer,
> To bring back a smile, to banish a tear?
>
> Not—"What was her shrine?" Nor—"What was
>   her creed?"
> But—"Had she befriended those really in need?"
> Not—"What was her way?"
> But—"How many were sorry when she
>   passed away?"
> For she left a good name that will remain always.[10]

---

10. As quoted in *Forever, Erma: Best-Loved Writing from America's Favorite Humorist* (Kansas City, Mo.: Andrews and McMeel, 1996), p. 249.

BOOKS FOR PROBING FURTHER

G od's wise words to us through His servant Solomon have indeed been "better than the profit of silver" and "more precious than jewels" (Prov. 3:14a, 15a). As you continue drawing upon the wealth of Proverbs and exploring the topics of our study further, we hope some of the following books will help make your efforts more precise and enriching.

The Book of Proverbs

Alden, Robert L. *Proverbs: A Commentary on an Ancient Book of Timeless Advice.* Grand Rapids, Mich.: Baker Book House, 1983.

Kidner, Derek. *The Proverbs: An Introduction and Commentary.* Tyndale Old Testament Commentaries series. Downers Grove, Ill.: InterVarsity Press, 1964.

Pursuing Wisdom

Bonhoeffer, Dietrich. *Meditating on the Word.* Translated and edited by David McI. Gracie. Cambridge, Mass.: Cowley Publications, 1986.

You and Your Tongue

Mains, Karen Burton. *You Are What You Say: Cure for the Troublesome Tongue.* Grand Rapids, Mich.: Zondervan Publishing House, 1988.

Mayhall, Carole. *Words That Hurt, Words That Heal.* Colorado Springs, Colo.: NavPress, 1986.

Virkler, Henry A. *Speaking Your Mind without Stepping on Toes.* Wheaton, Ill.: Scripture Press Publications, Victor Books, 1991.

You and Your Job

Briles, Judith, Luci Swindoll, and Mary Whelchel. *The Workplace: Questions Women Ask.* Today's Christian Woman Series. Carol Stream, Ill.: Christianity Today; Portland, Ore.: Multnomah Press, 1992.

Campolo, Tony. *Everything You've Heard Is Wrong*. Dallas, Tex.: Word Publishing, 1992.

Sherman, Doug, and William Hendricks. *Your Work Matters to God*. Colorado Springs, Colo.: NavPress, 1987.

Swindoll, Luci. *After You've Dressed for Success: A Guide to Developing Character as Well as a Career*. Waco, Tex.: Word Books, Publisher, 1987.

You and Your Counseling

Biebel, David B. *How to Help a Heartbroken Friend*. Nashville, Tenn.: Thomas Nelson Publishers, 1993.

Buchanan, Duncan. *The Counselling of Jesus*. The Jesus Library series. Downers Grove, Ill.: InterVarsity Press, 1985.

Crabb, Lawrence J., Jr. *Basic Principles of Biblical Counseling*. Grand Rapids, Mich.: Zondervan Publishing House, Ministry Resources Library, 1975.

―――. *Effective Biblical Counseling*. Grand Rapids, Mich.: Zondervan Publishing House, Ministry Resources Library, 1977.

―――. *Understanding People*. Grand Rapids, Mich.: Zondervan Publishing House, Ministry Resources Library, 1987.

D'Arcy, Paula. *When Your Friend Is Grieving: Building a Bridge of Love*. Wheaton, Ill.: Harold Shaw Publishers, 1990.

Swindoll, Charles R. *Encourage Me*. Portland, Ore.: Multnomah Press, 1982.

Some of the books listed above may be out of print and available only through a library. For those currently available, please contact your local Christian bookstore. Books by Charles R. Swindoll are available through Insight for Living. IFL also offers some books by other authors—please note the ordering information that follows and contact the office that serves you.

NOTES

NOTES

NOTES

NOTES

NOTES

NOTES

ORDERING INFORMATION

PROVERBS

If you would like to order additional study guides, purchase the cassette series that accompanies this guide, or request our product catalogs, please contact the office that serves you.

United States and International locations:

Insight for Living
Post Office Box 69000
Anaheim, CA 92817-0900

1-800-772-8888, 24 hours a day, seven days a week
(714) 575-5000, 8:00 A.M. to 4:30 P.M., Pacific time, Monday to Friday

Canada:

Insight for Living Ministries
Post Office Box 2510
Vancouver, BC, Canada V6B 3W7

1-800-663-7639, 24 hours a day, seven days a week

Australia:

Insight for Living, Inc.
General Post Office Box 2823 EE
Melbourne, VIC 3001, Australia

Toll-free 1800-772-888 or (03) 9877-4277, 8:30 A.M. to 5:00 P.M., Monday to Friday

World Wide Web:
www.insight.org

Study Guide Subscription Program

Study guide subscriptions are available. Please call or write the office nearest you to find out how you can receive our study guides on a regular basis.